COUNTER INTELLIGENCE

SMART, DELICIOUS RECIPES FROM MY FAMILY TO YOURS

THE BEST OF APRIL'S KITCHEN

BY APRIL HAMILTON

COUNTER INTELLIGENCE The Best of April's Kitchen
Copyright © by April Hamilton. All rights reserved.
Printed in Canada by Heritage Cookbook

ISBN 978-0-692-43096-5

Recipes, stories, and photographs by April Hamilton,
except Buckwheat Noodle Salad by Kenny Kemp and Roast
Chicken by Steve Payne Photography

Introduction

If I had to choose one word, one act, to improve health it would be this: Cook. Cooking is the key ingredient in the recipe for health. It is fun, engaging, economical, and it's never too late to get started.

The kitchen has always been my playground and the sound of a sizzling pan, the smell of delicious curling steam or the ding of the oven never fails to bring me joy. The youngest of 5 kids, I rarely strayed far from my mom, especially when it came to cooking. I learned my way around the kitchen alongside her at the counter, mesmerized with how she cooked breakfast (how can she spin the scrambled eggs in the bowl like that? Why don't they sling out onto the wall?), and helping pack my siblings' lunches. Once they left for school, my first question was always: 'what's for dinner?' I was offered the job of menu planning, anything to keep a preschooler out of a busy mother's hair. Taking inventory of our supplies, I'd offer my ideas for the evening family dinner. There was a simple formula to follow: a meat, a vegetable, and a starch. I floundered at first, but eventually my made-up menus were balanced enough to be served to the family. Nutrition 101 became a game that I was eager to master.

I remember pushing a kitchen chair to the stove to prepare my lunch, always soup from a can, usually tomato. I pretended to be Julia Child, mixing the soup with flair and a flurry of extra things – dried parsley flakes, chopped tomato, adding milk instead of water. I never tired of eating canned soup, doctoring up each batch with my signature. When I started off to school, we found a compact thermos and my soup creations followed me to school every single day.

My after-school hours were consumed with the kitchen. I'd cart cookbooks home from the book fair and check out only cooking titles at the library, constantly trying out new recipes. I invited friends over for playdates in the kitchen. I couldn't get enough.

In high school, my demonstration speeches were an opportunity to do mini cooking lessons with my classmates. My friend Aimee and I dazzled our Spanish class with Pollo de Barcelona and Leche Frita. (Aimee is the trained chef and dietitian whose nutrition tips are woven throughout this book.)

Off at college, my roommate called me Betty Crocker. She revealed that she had never eaten a home-cooked meal and together we started making a few simple recipes together: pasta with sauce, sugar cookies, salad dressing. I had the realization that growing up in the kitchen wasn't the norm, and introducing friends to cooking further fueled my passion.

Now a mother myself, the Nutrition 101 with my three daughters was automatic. Nothing forced, just kitchen fun with real food from the moment they arrived. Family dinner most nights, many hands, fresh ingredients, breaking bread at the table. They are all on board and have perfected their own specialties. When Sara left for college, she glanced at the stacks of books on the bench in the kitchen, "I'm going to miss the cookbooks," she confessed. Cooking is contagious.

Yes, it's my firm belief that a good meal can fix what ails you, and that cooking that meal with people you love, then sharing it together at the table, is the best part of the day. It doesn't have to be fancy.

Join me in the kitchen, to play, to savor. Belly up to the counter, invite your family and friends, and have fun! This book will show you the way to dozens of smart and delicious recipes, from the moment you awake, to soup and far beyond.

Happy Cooking!
April

FOREWORD

From the moment I heard it, I knew April Hamilton's book would be a success. She possesses a deep love and understanding of food, as well as the need to share that passion with others. Experiencing April's cooking instantly makes life better. Her guests are happier for having eaten her food and shared her passion for bringing the flavors out of ingredients to make them sing. This is an amazing gift.

The best dishes often have the simplest preparations that allow excellent ingredients, combined in flavorful and sometimes unexpected combinations, to shine through. This principle guides Counter Intelligence: The Best of April's Kitchen. The beautiful simplicity of April's cuisine makes for a cookbook that will be used again and again, for everyday meals and special occasions. Counter Intelligence is destined to become a cookbook that will, through stains and smudged pages, testify to years of delicious food shared with family and friends.

Cheers!
Nancy Bruns
chef and co-founder
JQ Dickinson Salt-Works, Malden, West Virginia

~~~~~~
~~~~~~

A Few Words From Aimee

"Of course," is what I said when April asked me to be a guest contributor to her upcoming brainchild, "Counter Intelligence, The Best of April's Kitchen". Her passion and commitment to helping others learn to cook or improve their kitchen skills while concocting recipes and perfecting ingredients is lifelong. She has special talent and incredible food knowledge which she happily shares. Every conversation with her amuses and inspires.

We both have had incredible influences in our lives which impacted our relationship with food and desire to cook wholesome, comforting food for ourselves and others. We were welcomed and encouraged in the kitchen. We shared family meals at the dinner table. There was an appreciation of nature's bounty and local ingredients. I think I can speak for April in that we will be forever grateful for these important values. It can be said, food is the truest expression of love and nurturing.

This mouth-watering compilation of recipes will provide readers with a simple approach to cooking in the home, while creating nourishing dishes to please all ages. When April was sending me recipes to provide nutrition tips, I could barely get through a day without giving one of the recipes a try.

Thank you to April for assembling a simply scrumptious assortment of recipes, tips, tricks and good advice. "Counter Intelligence, The Best of April's Kitchen" is sure to inspire and delight anyone who reads it. You will not go hungry. Your family and friends will surely thank you.

Enjoy!
Aimee Henry, RDN

TABLE OF CONTENTS

1

WIDE AWAKE

BREAKFAST BURRITO

BUTTERMILK PANCAKES

CRAZY GOOD
BREAKFAST SANDWICH

FRENCH TOAST

PERFECT BISCUITS

GRANOLA GOODNESS

TOAST YOUR TOAST

STRAWBERRY SMOOTHIE

AVOCADO TOAST

Ahh! Wide Awake! Time for Breakfast!

As family lore goes, there is an incident that echoes in my mind, as retold by my mother some hundreds of times. "Put your feet on the floor and cook me an egg!" came the command from one of her pint-sized kids, ordering her out of bed to make breakfast.

Though this happened long before I came along, I could imagine my oldest brother John, bossy toddler, blond curls bouncing as he stomped his little foot right on cue. No doubt my lovely mother obliged.

It's impolite to demand someone to make you breakfast, but the egg concept is a good one. Versatile, nourishing, and economical, eggs can be whipped into something amazing any time of day. We've all heard the news: breakfast is the most important meal of the day. Why deprive yourself? Set your alarm and make a habit of the morning meal.

Breakfast Burrito

Start with a batch of scrambled eggs, add a little pinch of cheese, and tuck it inside a warm tortilla for a great breakfast that is perfect for eating on the go. As my niece Kate says, "avocado on everything," and this is no exception. Layer a few slices of avocado before sliding your egg scramble onto the tortilla. Leftover grilled veggies also make a tasty addition. My husband loves crumbling a little bacon into his (is there ever leftover bacon?) If you choose to add a spoonful of salsa to your burrito, be sure to travel with extra napkins.

- 2 eggs
- Dash of salt
- Dash of pepper
- 1 teaspoon butter
- 2 tablespoons grated cheddar cheese (optional)
- 1 (8-10-inch) flour tortilla, preferably whole wheat

Optional toppings:
- Sliced ripe avocado
- Grilled vegetables
- One strip of bacon
- 1 tablespoon salsa

CRACK the eggs into a small bowl.
SPRINKLE in the salt and pepper and beat with a fork until yellow and frothy.
HEAT a small skillet (preferably cast iron or non-stick) over medium heat and melt the butter, swirling the skillet to coat the bottom of the pan. Add the eggs and cook until edges are set.
PUSH the eggs from outside edges to center of pan with a wooden spoon, scraping eggs off sides of pan as you stir.
ADD the cheese (if you are using it) and stir gently to combine and melt the cheese.
SLIDE the eggs onto the center of the warmed tortilla, top as desired.
FOLD the bottom of the tortilla up, then the sides, rolling carefully to hold it all together, and leaving the top open.

~~~~~~
~~~~~~

A Tip from Aimee – Refuel your brain and body after a good night's sleep. Studies show a well-balanced breakfast will kick still your metabolism and combat those mid-morning drops in mood and energy. Skipping meals, especially breakfast, can actually make weight control more difficult. Rise and shine with a healthy morning meal.

Buttermilk Pancakes

Homemade pancakes are so easy, no need for a mix! Buttermilk makes them tender. It's my most requested recipe, and a fun one for kids to master at an early age. When my daughter Emma was very small, she dragged a stool over to the stove and started pouring the batter on the griddle. "OOPS! Those are a little too close," I warned. But she knew exactly what she was doing-- making a Mickey Mouse shape. Encourage kids to make an "X" and an "O" with syrup to help as a 'serving size'.

- ½ cup all purpose flour
- ½ cup whole wheat flour
- 1 tablespoon sugar
- 1 teaspoon baking soda
- ½ teaspoon salt
- 1 cup buttermilk
- 1 egg
- 1 tablespoon vegetable oil
- Oil for the griddle
- Butter and maple syrup

NOTES regarding buttermilk:
1 - Some buttermilk is very thick. You may have to add a few tablespoons of regular milk if your batter is really thick
2 - To make your own buttermilk combine 1 tablespoon of white vinegar or lemon juice with 1 cup of milk.

COMBINE the flours, sugar, baking soda, and salt in a large mixing bowl and whisk together.

ADD the buttermilk, egg and oil to the dry ingredients and whisk together until smooth.

RUB a little oil over a griddle or large frying pan using a paper towel.

HEAT the griddle or large frying pan over medium heat.

POUR about 2 tablespoons of batter onto the heated griddle or frying pan for each pancake.

FLIP when the pancakes begin to bubble on the top and the bottom is golden brown. Don't rush the flipping or you'll just end up with a big mess. Cook the second side for about 1 minute.

SERVE. Butter and maple syrup are traditional toppings.

- To make blueberry pancakes, sprinkle a few blueberries on each pancake immediately after you have poured the batter on the griddle and cook as above.
- To make apple cinnamon pancakes, add 1 peeled, shredded apple and ½ teaspoon cinnamon to finished batter. Cook as directed above.

Yield: 12 4-inch pancakes

Crazy Good Breakfast Sandwich

At our house, 'crazy good' is a top-shelf rating given to something simple that actually knocks your socks off. It has become a competition of sorts in our kitchen and it goes like this: the designated cook whips up an unassuming dish – some pasta, a sandwich or a salad, nothing fancy – and gives it their taste-enhancing signature, usually something unexpected. The taster dives in and in 'eureka' fashion, shrieks, "this is crazy good!" You could also call it 'delicious plus delicious is delicious.' Have fun with your own crazy good creations!

- 2 slices whole grain bread
- 1 teaspoon pat of butter
- 1 egg
- Sprinkle of grated pepper jack cheese
- ¼ ripe avocado
- Pinch of salt and ground pepper

Some optional additions:
- Handful of fresh greens – spinach and arugula are crazy good
- Tomato slices
- Roasted bell peppers

TOAST the bread while you cook your egg.

HEAT a small skillet over medium heat and melt the butter, swirling the skillet to coat.

CRACK the egg into the skillet and sprinkle with salt and pepper.

COOK until the egg white looks set, about 2 minutes. Here comes the fun part...

FLIP the egg over and sprinkle with the cheese. (It takes a little practice, but you can lift the skillet and push it away from you, coaxing the egg toward the far edge of the skillet and flipping it up and over. Yes, fun! You can also flip it the old fashioned way with a spatula).

COOK until desired degree of doneness, about 1 minute for 'over easy' or a little longer for 'over medium'.

MASH the avocado with a fork onto one slice of toast.

TUCK some greens into the avocado, pressing in with the fork to help them stay put.

SLIDE the egg from the skillet onto the topped toast.

TOP with the other slice of toast, cut in half, and enjoy. (Or serve open-face if you prefer.)

Yield: 1 crazy good sandwich

French Toast

Leisurely weekend breakfasts are a relaxing way to bring everyone together, and French toast is perfect to serve to your family. Whether you have half a loaf of bread that isn't exactly sandwich worthy, or have a fresh loaf of challah dedicated to your dish, you will get rave reviews. Start with great bread and farm-fresh eggs. Each type of bread absorbs the egg batter differently, so just keep dipping and griddling until all the egg mixture is used up. Any leftovers freeze beautifully – just pop the cooled toasts into freezer bags and toast the frozen slices as needed for a quick workday breakfast.

- 2 eggs
- ½ cup milk
- 1 teaspoon ground cinnamon
- ½ teaspoon ground ginger (optional)
- 1 teaspoon vanilla extract
- 6 to 8 slices of bread (challah or cinnamon raisin bread are my favorites)
- 1 tablespoon butter
- Pure maple syrup or a sprinkle of powdered sugar for serving

CRACK the eggs into a small mixing bowl and whisk together with the milk, cinnamon, and vanilla extract. (Add ground ginger if you want a gingerbread twist).
TRANSFER the mixture to a pie pan or other flat dish with sides.
HEAT a heavy large skillet or griddle over medium heat and melt half of the butter in the skillet.
DIP bread into egg mixture, coating both sides, and immediately transfer to skillet (you may have to work in batches depending on the size of your skillet).
COOK until crisp and golden brown, about 2 minutes per side, adding butter as needed (a two-handed operation - lift the cooked slices of French toast with a spatula in one hand, and using a butter knife, smear a dab of butter on the skillet before turning the toast)
SERVE with maple syrup or a sprinkling of powdered sugar. If you are feeling luxurious, serve with a side of fresh fruit and maybe some bacon.

~~~~~~
~~~~~~

A Tip from Aimee – Studies suggest cinnamon may help to lower blood sugar in people with diabetes and it may have an effect on lowering cholesterol. Research around this distinctive spice is on-going. Stay tuned.

Granola Goodness

Be the Queen or King of breakfast and create a mountain of your own signature granola for your family (and friends!). This recipe is very adaptable to your personal preferences. It makes a ton, but can be adjusted easily by using less of everything or less (or none) of some of the things.

- 6 cups rolled oats (slow cooking)
- 2 cups sliced almonds
- 2 cups chopped pecans
- 1 cup coarsely chopped raw cashews
- 1 cup raw sunflower seeds
- ⅔ cup sesame seeds
- 1 cup raw pumpkin seeds
- ½ cup flax seed meal (or wheat germ)
- 2 tablespoons to ¼ cup brown sugar

- 1 tablespoon cinnamon
- ½ teaspoon salt
- ¾ cup oil (canola or sunflower)
- ¾ - 1 cup honey
- 2 teaspoons vanilla extract

Optional additions:
- 1 cup shredded coconut
- ¼ cup maple syrup (cut down honey by ¼ cup)
- 1 cup dried fruit (raisins, cherries, dates, other dried fruit)

Preheat oven to 325 degrees.
SPREAD oats on a large jelly roll baking pan.
BAKE for 15 minutes to toast.
COMBINE nuts, seeds, flax meal or wheat germ, brown sugar, cinnamon, and salt in a large bowl.
ADD toasted oats and optional coconut and mix well to blend.
HEAT oil and honey in a pan over medium low heat until it is liquidy but not boiling. Stir in vanilla (and optional maple syrup).
POUR warm liquid over oat-nut-seed mixture and mix well.
SPREAD mixture into an even mound on same baking pan used to toast oats and bake for 30-45 minutes, carefully stirring at 15-minute intervals, until light to deep golden brown.
REMOVE from oven and stir in your choice of dried fruit (optional)
COOL completely, then use spatula/pancake turner to remove it from the pan – I like to keep it in clumps.
STORE in airtight containers.

~~~~~~
~~~~~~

A Tip from Aimee – Granola is a great breakfast option. The fiber in oats helps to lower cholesterol and may reduce the risk of heart disease. Add extra cinnamon for more benefits.

Perfect Biscuits

My daughter Sara works in the after-hours cafe at college and decided to introduce biscuits from scratch to her customers. She reported rave reviews! "People have no idea how easy it is to make delicious biscuits! You have to put the recipe in your book," she insisted. So here you go. Easy, of course, and also flaky, with a tender interior. I made these when my friend Emily was visiting, and she confirmed Sara's suspicion –"I've never made biscuits from scratch." When I pulled the pan of golden goodness from the oven, Emily gasped, "I love you!" See for yourself and spread the love. Note – Grating the butter is a huge time saver. The cold strands of butter blend quickly with the dry ingredients and you are moments from biscuit bliss.

- 1½ cups unbleached all-purpose flour
- ½ cup whole wheat flour
- 1 tablespoon baking powder
- 1 teaspoon sugar
- ½ teaspoon salt
- ⅓ cup cold butter, preferably in one chunk cut from a whole stick
- ¾ cup milk

PREHEAT oven to 450 degrees.

TOSS together both flours, baking powder, sugar, and salt in a large bowl.

GRATE the butter over the flour mixture using the large holes of a cheese grater (or cut it into tiny dice). Mash together with a large fork until the mixture resembles coarse crumbs.

ADD the milk and stir gently until the mixture comes together and you can gather into a ball.

TRANSFER dough to a lightly floured surface and knead gently. PAT it out to a ¾" rectangle and cut into 2-3" rounds. Re-pat and cut remaining dough. Biscuits can also be cut into squares. Using a sharp-ish knife, cut the dough rectangle into 3 rows of 4 'squares' – no re-rolling is required and you get a fun shape!

ARRANGE 1" apart on a parchment-lined baking sheet and bake until puffed and golden, about 12-15 minutes, depending on the size.

SERVE warm with honey, jam, or just as-is. Hard to beat a piping hot flaky homemade biscuit.

Yield: 8-12 flaky biscuits

Strawberry Smoothie

Breakfast in an instant! When you might have hit snooze and time is tight, whip up a tasty smoothie for the ride into work. Line up the ingredients and let each person create their own personal blend. Strawberries are great, but feel free to play around depending on the fruits that you have on hand. Peaches make a delicious, creamy smoothie! West Virginia is renowned for its peach orchards – visit a U-Pick farm in the summer!

We love our 'Magic Bullet' blender, an inexpensive compact machine that blends right in the serving cup. If using a 'standard' blender, be sure to layer the ingredients beginning with the liquids for the best blending experience.

- ⅔ cup plain yogurt*
- ⅓ very ripe banana, peeled, sliced and frozen**
- 6 fresh strawberries, well rinsed, and hulled (frozen berries are great, too!)
- ⅓ cup orange juice
- Honey, to taste, just a teaspoon or two
- Ice cubes, if using fresh fruit

PUT the yogurt in the container of a blender.
ADD the banana slices, berries, orange juice, and honey.
PUT the lid securely on the blender
BLEND on high speed until smooth. With the machine running, remove the center part of the blender lid and drop in a few ice cubes and blend until ice is crushed.
SERVE with a smile!
FREEZE any leftover smoothie in ice pop molds or small paper cups for smoothie pops. (See the 'In Between' chapter for some great ideas)

*I like to use Greek yogurt — it has double the protein and calcium of 'regular' yogurt. Plain Greek yogurt is available in large containers, but be sure to choose the fat-free or low-fat variety — the 'full fat' type is very high in fat...not what you want in a fruity refreshing smoothie!

**Hold on to those blackening bananas! Rather than toss your over-ripe bananas, peel and slice them and lay them on a wax-paper-lined cookie sheet. Freeze them, then bag the frozen banana chunks into freezer bags — ready for smoothies any time.

Yield: 1-2 servings

Toast Your Toast

This is not so much a recipe as a concept: Make a morning meal out of a great slice of toast. Sounds pretty basic, but you can jazz up your slice according to your mood and what's on hand. I'm always happy to have ripe avocados at the ready, and I smear the green goodness right onto a darkly toasted slice of whole grain bread. Sprinkle with a pinch of coarse salt and a shower of fresh herbs and ordinary becomes extraordinary. In a decadent mood? Put together a tasty sandwich featuring fresh strawberries, dark chocolate, and almond butter. Enjoy this any time of day!

In my town, we have a fantastic bakery that serves up beautiful loaves and makes topping up toast for breakfast a no-brainer. On that note, I'd like to toast Libby and her team of talented bakers at Charleston Bread for making mornings so delicious! Toast the bakers in your town.

AVOCADO TOAST
- 1 slice grainy bread, darkly toasted
- ½ ripe avocado
- Pinch of salt and ground pepper
- Minced fresh herbs, such as cilantro, parsley or basil

CHOCOLATE-STRAWBERRY-ALMOND BUTTER TOAST
- 2 slices whole wheat bread, freshly toasted
- 1 tablespoon dark chocolate chips
- 1 ½ tablespoons almond butter
- 2 strawberries, hulled and sliced

AVOCADO TOAST
SCOOP the avocado half from the skin and lay the avocado directly on the warm toast.

SMASH the avocado with the tines of a fork to spread it across the toast.

SPRINKLE with a little salt and pepper and shower with fresh herbs.

ENJOY!

CHOCOLATE-BERRY-ALMOND BUTTER TOAST SANDWICH
SPRINKLE the chocolate chips on one slice of the warm toast and quickly top with the other slice of toast to melt the chocolate.

REMOVE top toast and spread the less-chocolatey slice of toast with the almond butter.

LAY strawberry slices into the almond butter in one layer and top with the chocolate-covered toast.

CUT the sandwich in half and enjoy!

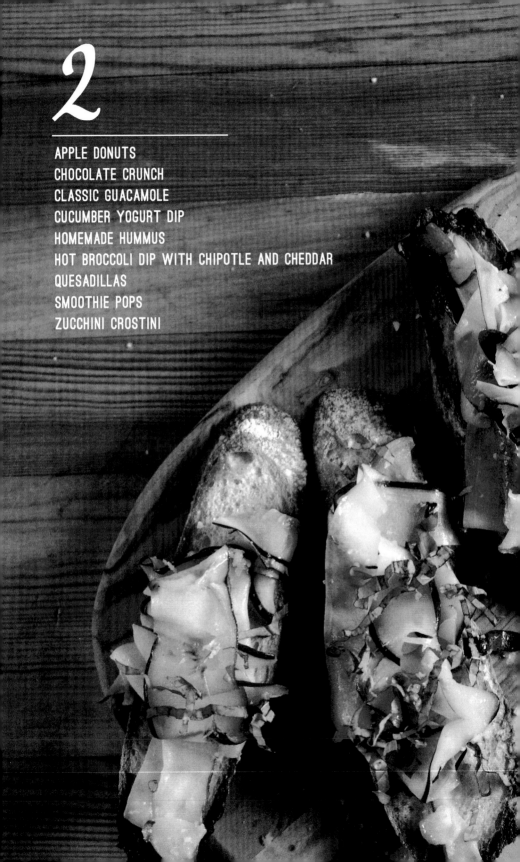

2

in
Between

APPLE DONUTS

CHOCOLATE CRUNCH

CLASSIC GUACAMOLE

CUCUMBER YOGURT DIP

HOMEMADE HUMMUS

HOT BROCCOLI DIP WITH CHIPOTLE AND CHEDDAR

SMOOTHIE POPS

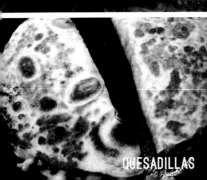

QUESADILLAS

ZUCCHINI CROSTINI

Always With You...Healthy Snacks!

Always keep a healthy snack handy for that time of day when you need a little something before lunch, or a tasty, satisfying bite after school or work. Being prepared is the key to banish the growling stomach before caving in to the call of the vending machine. Keep a portion of Chocolate Crunch as a tasty gym bag pick-me-up or pre-lunch nibble. It's satisfying and crunchy with a protein boost from nuts and whole grains. Whip up a batch of Cucumber Yogurt Dip and prep some veggies so you'll have this ready before the crash.

Snacking is often a guilty pleasure, but these won't weigh you down in between meals.

My friend Ali calls it "that 15-minute window to get food in." These smart recipes will have you prepared when snack attack arrives.

Apple Donuts

A favorite snack at our house, apple donuts are remarkable and so satisfying. You thinly slice your apples crosswise and remove the circular core from the center. Voila! No frying, no sugary coating. Just crunchy apple slices that look like a donut. All credit here goes to my brilliant husband for inventing this remarkable treat.

- Apples, use your favorite variety; each one provides 8-10 slices

Optional:
- Lemon juice to preserve them for a short time if they are not going to be eaten immediately

SLICE apple crosswise with a sharp knife and remove the circular core from the center.
SERVE and enjoy immediately!
RUB slices with small amount of lemon juice if they are not going to be served immediately. They will brown if not eaten right away.

~~~~~~
~~~~~~

A Tip from Aimee – This is one fruit where you may taste a difference between organic and conventional. Do a taste test and experiment with different varieties to find ones that please you and your family. Apples are the perfect snack to help stave off hunger as they contain lots of fiber to help you feel full and satisfied until your next meal. Add a bit of peanut butter to up the protein and you will be good to go.

Chocolate Crunch

This is a great snack! You combine the 'heart-healthy' benefits of dark chocolate with whole grain cereal and nuts and fruit — it's crunchy and a little sweet and fun to make and eat! I love to add dried cherries which give a tangy and chewy contrast to the sweetness of the chocolate and the crunch of the cereal and nuts.

Pack the cooled mixture into go-containers or snack bags and it's ready to go for a hike or as a lunchbox or gym bag nibble.

- ½ cup sliced almonds
- ¼ cup pumpkin seeds
- ¼ cup sunflower seeds
- ½ cup bittersweet chocolate chips, melted
- 3 cups multi-grain squares cereal
- 1 cup dried cherries or dried cranberries

HEAT oven to 350 degrees.
SPREAD the almonds, pumpkin seeds and sunflower seeds on a rimmed baking sheet and toast in the oven for 7 minutes.
MELT the chocolate in a small microwavable glass bowl for about one minute, stirring at 30 second intervals. (Or place in the top of a double boiler over hot, but not boiling, water. Stir until melted.)
COMBINE the toasted nut mixture with the cereal squares and dried fruit in a large bowl.
DRIZZLE with the melted chocolate and stir gently to combine.
SPREAD the mixture on a wax paper-lined baking sheet and refrigerate until the chocolate is set, about 30 minutes.
STORE in an airtight container, or put individual servings into snack bags.

~~~~~~
~~~~~~

A Tip from Aimee – Go nuts! Seeds and nuts contain phytosterols which are plant based compounds similar in structure to cholesterol. When consumed in sufficient amounts they are believed to reduce blood levels of cholesterol. Of the seeds and nuts typically consumed as snack foods, sunflower seeds and pistachios contained the most phytosterols, followed by pumpkin seeds.

Classic Guacamole

There is a very good reason that this popular dip ends in 'OLE'! No fiesta would be complete without the company of this festive dip. Spoon it into lettuce 'boats' as a satisfying finger food. It's no-goo when you can scoop the soft green goodness right from its shell and into a bowl and start smashing. The hardest part of perfect guacamole is having your avocados 'just right'. See Aimee's tip, below and the 'Smart Kitchen' chapter for more information about avocados.

- 2 medium avocados, ripened/soft
- Juice of 1 lime
- ½ teaspoon coarse salt
- Small firm lettuce leaves or tortilla chips for dipping

Optional add-ins:
- Red onion, finely chopped
- Tomato, diced
- Jalapeño, minced
- Fresh cilantro, chopped

CUT the avocados in half, running your knife around the pit from stem to blossom end and back up again.

TWIST the halves in opposite directions to free the pit, and pull the halves apart.

DISLODGE the pit, then scoop the avocado out of the 'shell' into a medium bowl.

MASH the avocado with a large fork or potato masher, and stir in the lime juice and salt. Add your choice of add-ins and stir gently.

SERVE with small, firm lettuce leaves for dipping or with tortilla chips. Get ready for raves of 'OLE'!

Note – If not using immediately, cover with plastic wrap pressed directly on the surface of the guacamole. Refrigerate for up to 2 days.

~~~~~~
~~~~~~

A Tip from Aimee – Unlike other fruits and vegetables, avocados are high in fat – mainly healthy, monounsaturated fats. This fruit contains nearly 20 essential nutrients and also acts as a booster by helping you absorb fat-soluble nutrients like vitamins A, D, E, and K. The creamy consistency makes it one of the first fresh foods a baby can enjoy.

Cucumber Yogurt Dip

Creamy yogurt dances with fresh herbs and cooling cucumber for a great in between snack. Many cultures serve up a version of this popular dip – in Morocco they top meatballs with it, and it's known as Raita in Indian cuisine, a cooling side to tame their spicy dishes. In Turkey and Greece it's called Tzatziki. No matter the name, keep this on hand as a regular go-to with grainy crackers or crisp carrot and cucumber slices. It's a great addition to a lunch box – be sure to pack it with an ice pack.

- 1 medium cucumber
- 1 cup plain yogurt
- 1 tablespoon minced fresh herbs (a combo of dill, mint, and basil is nice)
- 1 green onion, finely minced
- ¼ teaspoon salt
- Pinch of cayenne pepper

PEEL the cucumber and cut it in half lengthwise. Scrape out the seeds using a spoon.

CHOP the cucumber into tiny pieces, or you can shred it on the large holes of a cheese grater.

COMBINE the yogurt with the cucumber in a medium bowl.

ADD the minced herbs and green onion, and season with salt and cayenne pepper if desired, and stir well to combine.

CHILL until ready to serve. Keeps for up to 5 days in the refrigerator.

~~~~~~
~~~~~~

A Tip from Aimee – A word on yogurt… This is one of those items where it is very important to read the nutrition facts label on the container. Look for the most healthful option by choosing a brand that is high in protein, with no or low fat, and with no or few added sugars. As a general rule, look for less than 10mg of added sugar per serving.

Homemade Hummus

It can be tempting to toss a container (or two) of hummus into your shopping cart, but once you make your own custom blend, you will be hooked on homemade. It's effortless to whip up hummus at home and costs significantly less than store-bought. Give your hummus your signature tweak – extra lemon, less garlic, fresh herbs, something spicy. You get to choose. Once you master it, you can make it without a recipe and you'll always want to keep some on hand. Spread it on a sandwich, dip fresh carrots or pita chips. It's a perfect power snack, packed with protein.

- 2 cloves garlic, peeled
- 1 (15-ounce) can chick peas, drained and rinsed
- Zest and juice of 1 lemon
- ½ cup boiling water
- 2 tablespoons olive oil, plus extra for storing
- ½ teaspoon coarse salt
- Pinch of red chili flakes

PULSE the garlic in a food processor to mince.
ADD the drained chick peas, lemon zest and juice and boiling water.
BLEND for 3 minutes, scraping the side of the container after 1 minute.
ADD the olive oil, salt, and red chili flakes and blend until smooth.
TRANSFER to an airtight container and drizzle the top with a bit of olive oil to keep from drying out.
REFRIGERATE for up to 1 week.
Note – 'Authentic' hummus contains tahini, a nutty paste made from sesame seeds. Once when I was out of tahini, I made my hummus without it and pumped up the flavor with extra lemon juice.

~~~~~~
~~~~~~

A Tip from Aimee – What's that smell? Allicin is the bioactive compound found in garlic which gives it its distinctive smell. Greater health benefits are achieved when the garlic cloves are chopped or crushed which releases the allicin. Research has shown an association between garlic consumption and decreased risk for certain types of cancers like esophageal, stomach, colon, and pancreatic. Too much garlic may interfere with certain medications and cause stomach upset. One clove a day should do the trick – and keep the vampires away, too!

Hot Broccoli Dip with Chipotle and Cheddar

Move over, kale! Broccoli goes uptown with this fabulous dip. Serve with crostini (see recipe in 'Pantry' chapter) as a delicious dip for a festive starter. Prepare it in advance and it's ready to heat when hunger strikes.

- 1 large head broccoli, outer stalks trimmed to remove the tough layer
- 2 tablespoons butter
- 2 tablespoons flour
- 1 cup milk (skim works great)
- 1¼ cups shredded sharp cheddar cheese, divided
- 1 teaspoon minced canned chipotle chiles in adobo (see 'Smart Kitchen' chapter for info)
- Salt to taste

HEAT oven to 350 degrees.
CHOP the broccoli in batches in the food processor, pulsing to make small bite-size pieces, or chop by hand.
MELT the butter in a large saucepan over medium heat.
WHISK in the flour and cook, stirring, for 2 minutes.
ADD the milk and stir constantly until thickened and bubbling.
REMOVE from the heat and whisk in 1 cup of the cheddar and the chipotle. Add salt, to taste, and more chipotle, if desired.
MIX the broccoli into the cheese sauce and transfer to a buttered 1½-quart shallow baking dish.
BAKE for 20 minutes, until heated through.
SPRINKLE top with remaining ¼ cup cheese. Continue baking for 5 minutes to melt the cheese, or broil for 2 minutes until bubbling and golden.

~~~~~~
~~~~~~

A Tip from Aimee – Shred your own cheese if you have a few extra minutes. There is a difference between block cheeses and pre-shredded varieties. Pre-shredded cheese performs differently in recipes because it has been treated with anti-clumping and anti-mold agents. Also, when you grate your own cheese you get about twice as many shreds by volume compared to factory shredded, so it is far more cost effective. Remember, almost everything tastes better when you've labored over it yourself.

Quesadillas

Mexican-style grilled cheese! It is so easy to melt a bit of cheese inside a tortilla and call it a meal. You can add in all sorts of delicious things to add your signature to this tasty griddled treat. (We have certainly had a 'crazy good' quesadilla creation emerge from our kitchen!) Top it with some guacamole and you're set. I never realized this was recipe-worthy until people actually asked for the recipe. Grating your own cheese is key. Grab your grater (or better yet, grab your kids who can grate away!) and start griddling.

- 1 10-inch flour tortilla (preferably whole wheat)
- ¼ cup (1 ounce) grated cheese (cheddar or Monterey Jack)
- A little olive oil (about 1 teaspoon per quesadilla)
- Dollop of guacamole and/or salsa for topping

Optional Fillings:
- Chopped green chiles
- Canned black beans (drained and rinsed)
- Frozen corn kernels (thawed)
- Sliced green onions
- Grilled vegetables
- Cooked chicken (those leftovers from Fiesta night!)

BRUSH a little olive oil on one side of tortilla.
PLACE tortilla, oiled side down, in a large skillet over medium heat.
SPRINKLE half of cheese on one half of tortilla. Add optional fillings on top of cheese and top with remaining cheese.
FOLD the empty side of tortilla over the cheese and fillings using a spatula.
COOK for about 2 minutes on each side or until the cheese melts and tortilla is golden brown.
TRANSFER to a plate and let cool for about 2 minutes.
CUT into triangles.
SERVE as is or top with a dollop of guacamole and/or salsa.

DID YOU KNOW…grating your own cheese is fun and easy! The packaged shredded cheeses are typically more expensive, and they also have a coating of 'cellulose' that keeps the cheese shreds from sticking together and prevents the delicious results you are looking for… (No thanks! I'll grate it myself!)

Smoothie Pops

So, you've blended a beautiful fruit smoothie for breakfast. You pour it into your go-cup and there's a bit remaining in your blender. Rather than tossing the whole thing into the sink, pour up the extra smoothie into Popsicle molds and pop them in the freezer.

You will be delighted to find a quick snack ready when hunger hits. Frosty, fruity, and refreshing.

No popsicle molds? Instead, use paper cups and wooden popsicle sticks.

• Recipe for Strawberry Smoothie (see recipe in the 'Wide Awake' chapter, or concoct your own blend)
• Popsicle molds
OR
• Paper cups and wooden popsicle sticks

Optional additions to jazz up your creation:
• Sliced berries
• Kiwi

POUR the smoothie mixture into the molds, leaving room at the top for expansion in the freezer. If using cups, cover the cups with foil and insert wooden Popsicle sticks through the foil. The foil will keep the sticks in place. FREEZE for at least 4 hours.
ENJOY!

Zucchini Crostini

Zucchini is one of the prominent staples that could lose its appeal if not for the countless cooking methods that highlight its versatility. A personal favorite is zucchini ribbons. You simply scrub the zucchini, trim the ends off, and use your vegetable peeler to turn it into a pile of paper thin strips. Quick-saute the strips in some fragrant olive oil, season with fresh garlic, herbs, and a squeeze of lemon. You instantly have a flavorful side dish. A sandwich topping. A quesadilla filling. You get the idea. These tasty crostini convert even the most vegetable-averse diner every time! A pint-sized cooking class student remarked, "she makes the things that I don't like taste good!"

- 4 zucchini
- 1 tablespoon olive oil
- 4 cloves minced garlic
- 1 pinch red chili flakes
- Zest and juice of ½ lemon
- Coarse salt and freshly ground black pepper
- 2 tablespoons freshly chopped herbs (parsley and basil pair well)
- Baguette, sliced diagonally and grilled or toasted to make crostini

TRIM the ends of the zucchini and using a vegetable peeler, thinly slice the zucchini lengthwise.
HEAT the olive oil in a large skillet over medium high heat.
SAUTE the zucchini ribbons until lightly golden and wilted, about 3 or 4 minutes.
ADD the garlic and chili flakes, and cook 1 minute longer.
ADD the lemon zest and juice, and salt and pepper, to taste.
SPRINKLE in the fresh herbs and toss to combine.
SERVE on crostini, diagonal slices of baguette that have been grilled or toasted (see recipe in the 'Pantry' chapter).

~~~~~~
~~~~~~

A Tip from Aimee – When purchasing zucchini look for ones which are of average length but heavy for their size. The rind should be shiny and unblemished. A hard rind may indicate the squash is over-mature containing tough seeds and stringy flesh. Store these veggies unwashed in an airtight container in the fridge. Try not to overcook as the flesh will get mushy and nutrients will be lost.

Notes

3

SOUP
AND
BREAD

SWEET POTATO CHILI

NEW SCHOOL ALPHABET SOUP

CARROT GINGERSOUP

CILANTRO LIME SOUP

FRENCH ONION SOUP WITH MUSHROOMS

TOMATO BASIL BISQUE

SARA'S SUNSET SOUP

TURKEY MOLÉ CHILI

Bread Goes Great With Soup...

Hand in hand, soup + bread = perfect partners to make a meal. In my youth, canned soup was king and I always accompanied my concoction with a bite of bread for dipping. Now I make my own because it's so easy and few things comfort like homemade soup.

Start with sauteed onions, add your seasonings, some vegetables and maybe some meat, and homemade stock (a no-brainer, check the 'Pantry' chapter), suddenly you have soup. Make a huge batch and freeze some for later, or scale back and make a quick pot for 2. Add a delicious bread from your neighborhood bakery – or try baking some of your own!

Naturally delicious, from scratch, with love. Soup!

Carrot Ginger Soup

Bright carrots dance with fragrant ginger to make a soothing pot of delicious soup. My friend Amy sipped her first spoonful and exclaimed, "OHHH! This is like OHHH OHHHHHH! This is better than chocolate!"
Share the OHHH!

- 2 tablespoons olive oil
- 1 onion, chopped
- 1 clove garlic, crushed or minced
- 1 tablespoon minced fresh ginger
- 4 large carrots (about 1 lb. preferably organic), peeled and thinly sliced
- 4 cups chicken or vegetable stock (I typically use vegetable)

HEAT the olive oil in a large saucepan over medium heat.
ADD the onion and saute for 5 minutes to soften.
ADD the garlic and ginger and saute 1 minute (enjoy the fragrance!)
ADD the sliced carrots and cook for 5 minutes to soften.
ADD 3 cups of the broth and bring to a boil.
REDUCE heat and simmer for 20 minutes or until carrots are tender
PUREE soup in batches (blender or food processor), or in the pot with an immersion blender.
RETURN soup to the pot and heat, adding additional broth if needed.
SEASON with salt to taste (depending on saltiness of broth).
LADLE into bowls and serve.

~~~~~~
~~~~~~

A Tip from Aimee – Not only does it add zing and zip and a great aroma to a recipe, ginger has been shown to have medicinal properties. Eating this fragrant root in various forms can soothe an upset stomach.

Cilantro Lime Soup

This is summer in a bowl. Cilantro-infused broth with a tangy twist of lime and lots of veggies. It's a virtual trip to the shores of sunny Mexico.

* 2 tablespoons olive oil
* 1 onion, chopped
* 2 garlic cloves, minced
* 1 tablespoon chili powder
* 2 skinless boneless chicken breast halves, cut into ¾-inch pieces
* 5 cups chicken stock
* 1 cup fresh or frozen corn kernels
* 1 medium zucchini, diced
* 1 (14-ounce) can diced tomatoes, preferably fire-roasted
* ½ bunch fresh cilantro sprigs, tied together with kitchen string

AFTER IT'S SOUP
* ¼ cup chopped fresh cilantro
* ¼ cup fresh lime juice
* Diced avocado and lime wedges for serving

HEAT oil in heavy large saucepan over medium heat.
ADD onion and sauté until slightly softened, about 5 minutes.
ADD garlic and chili powder, and stir 1 minute
ADD chicken, and stir 2 minutes
ADD broth, corn, tomatoes, zucchini, and ½ bunch cilantro sprigs to saucepan.
BRING to boil.
REDUCE heat and simmer until chicken is cooked through, about 10 minutes.
DISCARD cilantro sprigs.
ADD chopped cilantro and lime juice to soup.
SEASON with salt and pepper.
LADLE into bowls and garnish as desired.

~~~~~~
~~~~~~

A Tip from Aimee – Cilantro is essential in many ethnic cuisines. To keep your cilantro happy after purchase, place the stems in a glass of water and store in the refrigerator with a loose plastic bag covering the leaves. While the leaves are most commonly used, the stems and roots are edible as well – save them to enhance the flavor of your soups and stocks.

French Onion Soup with Mushrooms

The classic version of this popular soup is made with beef stock. This one gets a rich flavor boost from homemade vegetable stock and fresh, sauteed mushrooms. It is luxury in a bowl, giving you the feeling that you're in an elegant restaurant when you're actually slurping soup in the comfort of home. Add a salad and you have dinner.

- 4 cups sliced onion (2-3 medium sized onions)
- 3 tablespoons olive oil
- 3 cloves garlic, minced or crushed
- 1 teaspoon salt
- 2 sprigs of fresh thyme
- $\frac{1}{2}$ pound fresh sliced mushrooms
- 2 tablespoons dry sherry
- $1\frac{1}{2}$ cups vegetable stock
- $3\frac{1}{2}$ cups chicken stock
- Ground black pepper
- 6 slices baguette or crusty bread, toasted or handfuls of homemade croutons
- $\frac{3}{4}$ cup grated Fontina or Swiss cheese

HEAT the olive oil in a large pot over medium heat.
SAUTE the onion, stirring occasionally until soft and golden, about 15 minutes. Add the garlic, salt, and whole thyme sprigs and cook for 1 minute.
STIR in the mushrooms and cook, stirring occasionally until mushrooms are soft, about 10 minutes.
INCREASE heat to medium high and add the sherry and cook for 1 minute.
ADD the vegetable stock and chicken stock and bring to a boil.
REDUCE heat to medium-low and simmer for 15-20 minutes. Season with pepper and additional salt if needed.
LADLE the soup into 6 heat-proof bowls (be sure they can be used in a broiler) and top each with a baguette toast. Sprinkle each with some of the cheese and place the bowls on a rimmed baking sheet.
HEAT the broiler and carefully slide the sheet of soupbowls underneath the broiler.
BROIL until the cheese melts and bubbles, 1-4 minutes, depending on your oven.

Yield: 6 servings

New School Alphabet Soup

My friend Nicole and her son Gabe love this soup! It's practically a spelling lesson right at the kitchen table. Is that why Nicole loves it? (It's simply delicious...I know that's why Gabe loves it.) Other tiny pasta can be used — try orzo, ditalini, or stars. However...kids seem to overlook any unwelcome green things when they can spell words in their bowl of homemade soup.

- 2 quarts chicken stock
- 1 (14-ounce) can whole tomatoes, crushed with your hands (rip them right over the pot!)
- 2 garlic cloves, minced or crushed
- 1 onion, finely chopped
- 1 (15-ounce) can chick peas, drained and rinsed
- 2 large handfuls fresh spinach, roughly chopped
- Handful of fresh basil leaves, finely chopped
- ½ cup alphabet pasta
- Salt and pepper to taste
- Parmesan cheese for serving, if desired

COMBINE in a large pot the broth, tomatoes and their juices, and the garlic and onion. Bring to a boil, then reduce heat.
ADD the chick peas and spinach
SIMMER 20 minutes.
STIR in the basil and pasta, salt and pepper, to taste, and simmer for 6 minutes or so (depending on type of pasta), until the pasta is tender.
LADLE into bowls and top with cheese.

~~~~~~
~~~~~~

A Tip from Aimee – Soups are a great vehicle for adding vegetables to your diet and using leftovers. It has been shown, people typically consumed fewer calories on days when they ate soup rather than eating the same ingredients in solid form. Soup has a high water content and veggie-packed soups are high in fiber, both which help you to feel full. Bottom Line: Soups are satisfying. Go for broth-based over cream-based.

Sara's Sunset Soup

I created this recipe years ago for an 'Easy Weeknight Meals' cooking class, and it's been a family favorite ever since. My daughter Sara gave the flavorful concoction its name "because it's all red and yellow like the sunset". It tastes like the sunset, too, with a spicy warmth from curry powder and a lift from fresh lemon.

It can be thrown together in minutes, making it a great go-to on busy weeknights. Your junior kitchen helpers can crush the garlic, squeeze the lemon, and, age depending, chop potatoes and herbs. Kitchen fun together followed by the relaxing finale of sitting down and enjoying comfort in a bowl. Add some crusty bread and a nice salad and you have a feast that's just right, and easy for a weeknight.

- 2 tablespoons vegetable oil
- 1 small onion, finely chopped
- 3 large garlic cloves, minced or crushed
- 1½ teaspoons curry powder, or more or less to taste
- 1 (14½-ounce) can diced tomatoes with juice
- 1 (15-ounce) can chickpeas, drained and rinsed
- 1 medium potato, scrubbed and diced
- 4 cups chicken stock or vegetable stock
- 1 tablespoon lemon juice
- 2 tablespoons chopped fresh cilantro

HEAT the oil in a large saucepan over medium heat, .
ADD the onion and cook until slightly softened, about 5 minutes.
ADD the garlic and curry powder and stir 1 minute.
ADD the tomatoes with their juices and boil for 5 minutes, until slightly reduced and thick.
STIR in the chickpeas, potato and stock and simmer until the potatoes are tender, about 20 minutes, stirring occasionally.
STIR in the lemon juice and cilantro. Season to taste with salt.
LADLE into bowls and serve with a smile.

~~~~~~
~~~~~~

A Tip from Aimee – Look for low sodium options when purchasing canned goods. Rinsing canned beans before using will eliminate some of the excess sodium.

Sweet Potato Chili

Meatless Monday is a smart concept to promote going 'meat-free' part-time. This bold chili is a perfectly delicious way to enjoy your meat-free day and it's proudly endorsed by kids! My friend Jeannie's son Samuel asked if he could add the recipe to his classroom cookbook.

This recipe easily doubles.

- 1 tablespoon olive oil
- 1 medium onion, chopped
- 2 teaspoons ancho chili powder
- 1 cup vegetable stock or water
- 1 large red-skinned sweet potato, peeled, cut into ¾-inch chunks
- 1 (14½ -ounce) can diced tomatoes, preferably fire- roasted
- 1 (15-ounce) can black or pinto beans, drained and rinsed
- 3 tablespoons chopped fresh cilantro
- Zest of 1 orange

HEAT olive oil in a medium saucepan over medium heat.
ADD onion and sauté until slightly softened, about 5 minutes.
ADD chili powder and stir 1 minute.
ADD broth and sweet potato chunks.
COVER pan; reduce heat and simmer 10 minutes.
ADD tomatoes with their juices and the beans.
SIMMER uncovered until chili thickens and sweet potato is very tender, about 10 minutes.
MIX in cilantro and orange zest and season to taste with salt and pepper.
LADLE into bowls and serve.

~~~~~~
~~~~~~

A Tip from Aimee – Did you know the zest of citrus fruits contain 5 to 7 times more nutrients than the juice? Citrus peels contain flavonoids which have anticancer, antidiabetic, and anti-inflammatory properties. Another benefit… the refreshing fragrance when zesting an orange can perk you up!

Tomato Basil Bisque

It's a classic comfort food, adored by all. Adding just a splash of milk at the end of cooking gives a slight creamy nuance while still keeping a healthy profile. Calling it 'bisque' takes it from simple to uptown. Pack it in a thermos for an excellent lunch on the go. Chase a gray day away with a pot of homemade soup! Add some fresh baby spinach at the end of cooking to make a Florentine variation.

- 1 tablespoon butter or olive oil
- ½ cup finely chopped onion
- 2 cloves garlic, finely chopped
- 1 small carrot, grated
- 1 quart jar tomatoes, or 1 (28-ounce) can crushed tomatoes
- 2 cups vegetable stock
- ¼ cup milk
- Salt and pepper to taste
- Handful of fresh basil leaves, cut into thin strips

MELT butter or olive oil in a large saucepan over medium-low heat.
ADD onion and cook, stirring, until very soft, about 10 minutes.
ADD garlic and grated carrot and cook 1 minute.
ADD tomatoes and cook 10 minutes.
ADD stock and bring to a boil.
REDUCE heat, and simmer gently until thickened, about 20 minutes.
WHISK in milk and season with salt and pepper. Stir in basil.
LADLE into bowls and garnish with additional basil, if desired.

~~~~~~
~~~~~~

A Tip from Aimee – Basil is a highly aromatic herb packed full of vitamin K which is critical for healthy bones. Along with enhancing the flavor of dishes, adding fresh herbs provides numerous nutritional benefits. They are easy and fun to grow too – in the earth, a container garden, or a sunny window.

Turkey Molé Chili

We debuted this tasty chili at our cross country meet concession stand. It disappeared in record time! Adding just a hint of chocolate transforms it into a 'molé', a classic, festive Mexican dish. For a little smoky spice, add some chipotle. (See the 'Smart Kitchen' chapter for info regarding this spicy addition.)

- 1 tablespoon olive oil
- 1¼ pounds ground turkey
- 1 medium onion, chopped
- 4 cloves garlic, minced
- 1 carrot, peeled and finely grated
- 1 tablespoon ancho chili powder
- 1 tablespoon cocoa powder
- 1 teaspoon ground cumin
- ½ teaspoon dried oregano
- 1 teaspoon minced canned chipotle chiles in adobo (optional)
- 1 (28-ounce) can crushed tomatoes
- 2 tablespoons tomato paste
- ½ cup vegetable stock or water

- 1 teaspoon coarse salt (or to taste)
- ¼ teaspoon ground black pepper
- 1 (15-ounce) can black or pinto beans, drained and rinsed

Optional garnishes:
- Chopped green onion
- Jalapeño slices
- Shredded cheese

HEAT the oil in a large pot over medium heat.
ADD the onion and saute until softened, about 5 minutes.
ADD turkey and break it up with a spoon, stirring occasionally until no longer pink.
STIR in the garlic, carrot, chili powder, cocoa powder, cumin, oregano, and optional chipotle.
STIR for 1 minute to blend.
ADD the crushed tomato, tomato paste, and stock and season to taste with salt and pepper.
BRING to a boil, then reduce heat to low.
SIMMER for 20-30 minutes.
LADLE chili into bowls and top with desired garnishes.

Yield: 6 servings

4

GREAT

SALADS

BLT SALAD

BUCKWHEAT NOODLE SALAD

CARROT SALAD

FIESTA SALAD

REILLY'S DRESSED IN THE
BOWL CAESAR

SUNSHINE CITRUS SALAD

SWEET-SOUR-AND-SPICY
SWEET POTATO SALAD

A Great Side Dish or Light Meal

Accompany your plate with a fresh salad and suddenly your meal is complete. Colorful salads are the perfect side dish and an easy way to plug kids in to the kitchen. They are always eager to try new tastes when they have a hand in the prep. Let them man the salad spinner, peel carrots and cucumbers, rip a baguette for croutons.

What's in season? Add some farmers' market finds to your perfectly dressed greens. We've come a long way from watery iceberg.

The salads that follow are color-rich and flavor-full, and a great healthy addition to your menus.

BLT Salad

Thinking back, it seems like BLT night was the emergency meal when mom needed to make something quick with staples she kept on hand. Today, the sandwich is a decadent treat, gussied up on the menus in uptown restaurants. When summer tomatoes are at their peak, the classic sandwich unfolds beautifully on a bed of salad greens. Bacon, yes, from time to time. Crumble the real thing on top of your salad and dress it all up with buttermilk dressing. This salad is satisfying as a main course and is a total crowd-pleaser. Optional avocado marries harmoniously with the crisp bacon and tangy, creamy dressing. Cue niece Kate's "avocado on everything!" philosophy.

Cooking bacon in the oven is a kitchen saver – no spatters on your cooktop! Find the details in the 'Smart Kitchen' chapter.

HERBED BUTTERMILK DRESSING:
- ⅓ cup buttermilk
- ⅓ cup light sour cream
- ⅓ cup mayonnaise
- 2 tablespoons cider vinegar
- 1 tablespoon chopped flat-leaf parsley
- 1 tablespoon chopped fresh chives
- 1 clove garlic, minced or crushed
- ½ teaspoon coarse salt
- ¼ teaspoon freshly ground black pepper

WHISK together in a medium bowl, the buttermilk, sour cream, mayonnaise, vinegar, parsley, chives, garlic, and salt and pepper.
DRIZZLE 2 or 3 tablespoons of dressing over the salad.
STORE the dressing in an airtight container for up to 1 week.

FOR EACH SERVING OF SALAD:
- 2 large handfuls of freshest salad greens (romaine, spinach, red leaf, or a combination)
- 1 tomato, chopped or sliced
- 2 strips of crisply cooked bacon, chopped or crumbled
- ¼ avocado, chopped (optional)

LAY the greens out in a shallow serving bowl or large dinner plate.
TOP with the tomatoes and bacon, and optional avocado.
SERVE with the dressing, as described above.

Buckwheat Noodle Salad

Use your noodle and make a delicious salad highlighting the fresh flavors of Asian street food.

- 8 ounces buckwheat noodles
- 2 carrots, peeled and cut into matchsticks
- 1 tablespoon vegetable oil
- 1 tablespoon soy sauce
- 2 teaspoons honey
- 1 tablespoon rice vinegar
- Pinch red pepper flakes
- ¼ cup thinly sliced green onions
- 1 cucumber, peeled, cut in half lengthwise, seeded and chopped
- 1 tablespoon sesame seeds

COOK noodles according to package directions.
PREPARE carrots while water boils, placing them in the colander where you will drain the noodles.
DRAIN noodles on top of the carrot to cook slightly and carefully shake to remove all water.
WHISK the oil, soy sauce, honey, vinegar, and red pepper flakes together in a large serving bowl.
ADD the warm noodles and carrots and toss to combine.
STIR in the green onions and cucumber.
TOP the dish with sesame seeds
SERVE warm.

~~~~~~
~~~~~~

A Tip from Aimee – Did you know buckwheat is really not wheat at all? Despite its name, buckwheat is not a grass like wheat; it is more like a seed. This makes it safe for people with celiac disease or those who have gluten sensitivity. Check the label to make sure it's not processed in a plant with other gluten containing grains.

Carrot Salad

Whole fresh carrots keep for weeks in your crisper drawer and can save the day when you need a quick side salad. When there is no lettuce in sight, carrots save the day! Impressive enough for company, yet simple enough on a busy weeknight, well-dressed carrots are always a welcome partner on any dinner plate. Dress them according to your menu. A garlicky vinaigrette with fresh herbs suits many menus, but if you're going with an Asian theme, toss them with a ginger and sesame dressing. Mix and match and remember to save your washed carrot peels for your stock bag in the freezer (see the stock recipe in the 'Pantry' chapter).

- 4 large carrots, peeled
- 1 clove garlic, minced or crushed
- 1 tablespoon white vinegar
- 2 tablespoons olive oil
- 2 tablespoons minced fresh parsley
- Salt and pepper

GRATE the carrots using the large holes of a box grater or the shredding disk of a food processor.
COMBINE the garlic, vinegar, oil, and parsley in a medium bowl.
ADD the grated carrots to the dressing and season with salt and pepper.
TOSS to coat with the dressing.

~~~~~~
~~~~~~

A Tip from Aimee – Carrots contain carotenoids, a phytochemical, which may reduce the risk of cardiovascular diseases, certain cancers and age-related eye diseases. Eat vegetables and fruits that are red, orange and deep-green and chances are you'll be consuming carotenoids.

Fiesta Salad

You can have this festive salad when you're craving summer in the midst of winter, though it's at its best with Farmer's Market corn, and tomatoes from the garden. Make a little for tonight's side dish, or a huge bowl of it to impress the potluck revelers. It's easy to make and popular with everyone in the group! We were enjoying a summer evening on the patio and Iris and Zoe, my friend Cary's twin seven-year-olds, asked for the recipe. Of course! It's a party in a bowl.

- 1 (15-ounce) can black beans, drained and rinsed
- 1 cup corn kernels (from about 2 cooked or grilled ears, or frozen corn kernels, thawed)
- 2 green onions, chopped
- 2 plum tomatoes, chopped
- 1 tablespoon olive oil
- Zest of 1 lime
- 1 tablespoon lime juice
- 1 tablespoon chopped fresh cilantro
- ¼ teaspoon coarse salt
- 1 avocado, diced
- 1 small jalapeño, seeded and chopped, optional

COMBINE beans, corn, green onions, and tomatoes in a medium bowl.
STIR in the olive oil, lime zest and juice, cilantro and salt.
ADD the avocado and stir gently, adding jalapeño if desired.
SERVE as a salad, a festive dip for tortilla chips, a filling for a wrap...Spoon it into scoop-shaped tortilla chips for 2-bite tostadas.

~~~~~~
~~~~~~

A Tip from Aimee – Do you want to turn up the heat in the kitchen? Jalapeños are an easy and inexpensive way to add that spicy kick. Peppers derive their heat from a natural plant compound called capsaicin which has anti-inflammatory properties and acts as a vasodilator which promotes healthy blood flow. For those watching their waistline, capsaicin shows promise for weight loss by increasing energy expenditure after a meal.

Rainbow Coleslaw

Lightly dressed and bursting with color, this coleslaw is a wonderful partner to your plate. Serve alongside Sloppy Taco Dogs, as a topping for your Fiesta night fajitas, or with summer barbecue.

Any leftovers can be refrigerated for tomorrow's lunchbox.

- 1 tablespoon white or cider vinegar
- 1 tablespoon Dijon mustard
- 1 clove garlic, crushed or minced
- 2 tablespoons olive oil
- $\frac{1}{2}$ teaspoon salt
- $\frac{1}{4}$ teaspoon pepper
- $\frac{1}{2}$ head each red and green cabbage, cut in half, cored, and very thinly sliced
- 3 carrots, peeled and grated
- 2 green onions, thinly sliced

WHISK the vinegar, Dijon, and garlic in a large bowl. Slowly drizzle in the olive oil, whisking to blend and season with salt and pepper.

ADD the cabbage, carrot, and green onion.

TOSS well to evenly coat the salad.

SERVE, refrigerating any leftovers for up to 2 days.

~~~~~~
~~~~~~

A Tip from Aimee – Cabbage is considered a cruciferous vegetable like broccoli, cauliflower, kale, and Brussel sprouts and has been shown to be protective against cancer. Eat these greens, whites and purples raw or lightly steamed to retain the maximum health benefits. There are several types of cabbages – experiment and try varieties like savoy and bok choy (Chinese cabbage). Another bonus…they are less perishable than some of your other vegetables so they will last longer in the fridge after rinsing, draining, and placing in an airtight container or zippered bag.

Reilly's Dressed in the Bowl Caesar

When my daughter Reilly was 9, we made this salad on Good Morning West Virginia, the morning news show that precedes Good Morning America. Reilly wore her chef's outfit and entertained the viewers with her favorite recipe. She's in college now and the recipe is still in regular rotation.

SALAD
- Zest and juice of 1 lemon
- 1 head Romaine lettuce
- 1 teaspoon mustard
- 1 clove garlic, crushed or minced
- A pinch of salt and a few cracks of pepper.
- 3 tablespoons Extra Virgin olive oil
- ½ cup freshly grated Parmesan cheese

CROUTONS
- 1 baguette
- 2 tablespoons olive oil
- 3 garlic cloves, smashed

SALAD
WASH and dry the lettuce (a salad spinner is a big time saver!) Keep chilled until ready to serve.
MIX the lemon zest and juice, mustard, garlic, and salt and pepper in a large salad bowl.
WHISK in gradually the Extra Virgin olive oil, then add about 2 tablespoons Parmesan.
TEAR the lettuce and add it to the bowl.
TOSS the salad, then top with remaining Parmesan.
ADD croutons, if desired

GARLIC CROUTONS
TEAR baguette into bite-size pieces and place in a large bowl, drizzling with olive oil and tossing with garlic.
SPREAD on a baking sheet and season with salt and pepper.
BAKE at 350 for 10 minutes.
TOSS and turn the croutons and continue baking for 5-10 minutes longer until croutons are crunchy and golden.

Yield: 4 servings

Sunshine Citrus Salad

This delightful combination of fresh citrus is truly best made with Florida red grapefruit which are much tangier than other varieties – the sweetness of the orange balances very nicely with the tangy fruit. You can add halved red grapes for an extra burst of color. We traditionally serve this as our palate cleanser at Thanksgiving. It's a wonderful treat throughout the citrus season.

- 6 fresh red grapefruit, rinsed and dried
- 6 fresh navel oranges, rinsed and dried
- Small bunch of grapes, rinsed and cut in half (see Tomato Trick in the Smart Kitchen chapter), optional

TRIM the tops and bottoms off of the grapefruit and oranges using a very sharp knife.

SET the fruits on end, and carefully cut the skin from the flesh, beginning at the top and following the curves down. Rotate each fruit as you go, removing all of the peel with a bit of fruit clinging to it.

CUT out each section of the fruit by inserting the blade of the knife between the flesh and the membranes on both sides.* The wedges should come out easily, leaving only the membrane intact. As you cut, put all the fruit sections into a large bowl.

SQUEEZE the juice out of all the fruit membranes and peels (by hand) and add to the fruit.

COMBINE the fruit sections and their juice in a large bowl. Cover and refrigerate until ready to serve, adding grapes if desired.

SERVE in small dishes

Note: It is best to carefully cut the fruit over a bowl that will catch all the juice. If you prefer to safely cut on a cutting board, place the cutting board inside a shallow pan that will catch the juice – transfer the juice periodically to the bowl.

*The technique used to cut the citrus is called supreming.

Yield: 12 servings

Sweet-Sour-and-Spicy Sweet Potato Salad

Sweet potatoes are a beautiful backdrop for a little spice. This festive side dish is color-rich and full of flavor, with the added bonus that it's super easy to make. Slice and cook the sweet potatoes and toss with a warm dressing kissed with a jalapeño kick and you have a delicious warm sweet potato salad. It's a beautiful side for Thanksgiving. One taste and you'll wonder why the sweet potato-marshmallow pairing was ever invented.

- 4 large sweet potatoes, peeled, halved lengthwise, and sliced ¼-inch thick
- 1 medium onion, finely chopped
- 2 tablespoons olive oil
- 3 tablespoons fresh lime juice, divided use
- 1 jalapeño pepper, finely chopped
- 1 teaspoon coarse salt
- 2 tablespoons chopped fresh cilantro
- 2 green onions, thinly sliced

COOK sweet potato slices in a pot of boiling water until just tender, about 8 minutes. Drain.

HEAT the olive oil in a large skillet over medium heat and cook onion until very tender, about 10 minutes, stirring occasionally. (You can do this while the sweet potatoes are cooking).

ADD 2 tablespoons lime juice and stir to combine. (This will 'deglaze' the skillet.)

ADD cooked sweet potato, jalapeño, salt, and cilantro and gently toss together to blend flavors, adding additional tablespoon lime juice if desired.

TOSS in the green onions and serve warm.

~~~~~~
~~~~~~

A Tip from Aimee – Sweet potatoes are full of nutrients like potassium, vitamin A, and iron and are an excellent source of fiber. Adults need about 25-35 grams of fiber daily and most get less than 15 grams. A one-cup serving of sweet potatoes contains almost 7 grams of fiber. Aim to eat your fiber over the course of the day in meals and snacks, rather than loading up during one meal, and remember to increase your water intake as you bump up the fiber.

5

DINNER TABLE

ARTICHOKE CHICKEN

SKILLET LASAGNA

QUINOA PIZZA

ROAST CHICKEN

EMMA'S GREEN GODDESS PASTA

VEGGIE BURGERS

FAJITA FIESTA

NOODLE BOWL

All Hands at the Table...

Family dinner matters. I encourage you to come to the table, as families, to break bread, revisit the day's events and share a meal. Together.

All hands on deck for dinner prep makes for a fun and lively family experience, and gets dinner on the table in record time. Plan ahead, make multiple meals from one starter. Turn the potentially hectic time into a family-focused meaningful meal.

At our house, it's a no phone zone, glasses are raised, napkins in laps. They aren't usually linen napkins and the glasses don't always match, and certainly the silverware is hodgepodge, but it's our family and we are eating together, most nights.

Everyone pitches in, mostly, depending. We try to map out menus for the week, but often we just wing it. There are emergency supplies in the pantry: a good jar of sauce served over some al dente pasta, a bakery baguette from the freezer, salad greens. When our girls were little, they started helping in the kitchen with small tasks – making salad, stirring, flipping pancakes – and before long they gained lifelong kitchen skills. When we had a picky-eater dilemma, we employed the '5-star' category – recognizing and celebrating a dish that all five of us loved. The dish would become a regular in the menu rotation. Find some '5-star' recipes here.

Artichoke Chicken

Fast and Fantastic! I debuted this dish at a cooking class featuring quick weeknight meals and it's a winner. I try to keep cans of artichoke hearts in the pantry so I can whip this up at a moment's notice. It could hardly be easier. Mince some drained artichoke hearts and mix them with fresh garlic and tangy lemon zest and juice, a spoonful of mayo and some Parmesan. Spoon the artichoke goodness over boneless chicken cutlets and bake. In 25 short minutes, dinner's ready and your diners will be singing your praises.

Potatoes, bruschetta, quinoa or couscous would accompany this dish nicely. Add a green salad with radicchio and a simple vinaigrette and you're set!

- 2 boneless, skinless chicken breast halves, split horizontally into 2 cutlets each
- Salt and pepper
- 1 (14-ounce) can artichoke hearts, drained and chopped
- 2 tablespoons mayonnaise
- 1 tablespoon olive oil
- Zest of 1 lemon, plus 1 tablespoon juice
- 3 tablespoons Parmesan cheese, divided use
- 1 tablespoon minced fresh parsley or basil, plus additional for garnish

HEAT oven to 350 degrees.
SEASON chicken breast cutlets on both sides with salt and pepper.
PLACE in a shallow baking dish.
MIX together the artichokes, mayonnaise, olive oil, lemon zest and juice, 2 tablespoons Parmesan, and the minced parsley or basil in a small bowl.
TOP chicken breasts with artichoke mixture, dividing evenly.
SPRINKLE with remaining Parmesan.
BAKE until chicken is cooked through, about 25 minutes. To check doneness, cut into a piece of chicken at the center with a thin-bladed knife. The meat should be white or just slightly pink.

~~~~~~
~~~~~~

A Tip from Aimee – Sprinkle on the Parmesan sparingly. This hard, dry cheese is sharp, nutty, slightly salty and has intense flavor, and a little goes a long way, making it easier to eat in moderation. Just a little in recipes or grated on top at the finish of a dish adds big flavor without a lot of calories.

Emma's Green Goddess Pasta

Move over, marinara! This new topping for spaghetti, invented by my teenage daughter, is a velvety concoction that was her answer to the 'what's for dinner' dilemma.

Start with a ripe avocado. You know it's ripe when the skin darkens from bright green to dark almost black and the stem end is just barely soft. That's your clue to avocado perfection. Aaaaaaahhhvocado! Then blend it smooth with some milk and flavorful seasonings and you have 'Emma's Green Goddess'.

Once you master this addictive sauce, you'll want to put it on everything! From steamed fresh vegetables to crispy chicken cutlets, raw carrot sticks to salad greens, it adds an unexpected twist of silky complex flavor to anything in its company. Even those who are 'avocado-averse' can't seem to get enough.

Note – Always keep avocados on hand to whip up this easy dish!

- ½ cup milk (skim is great)
- 1 ripe avocado, pitted and scooped from the skin
- 2 cloves garlic, crushed
- ½ teaspoon coarse salt
- 1 tablespoon olive oil
- ¼ cup freshly grated Parmesan
- 2 tablespoons fresh lime juice
- 1 pound pasta, cooked to 'al dente' according to package directions, ½ cup cooking water reserved
- Additional Parmesan 'curls' for serving

POUR the milk into the container of a blender.
ADD the avocado, garlic, salt, olive oil, and Parmesan.
BLEND together until smooth (with the lid on). The mixture will be quite thick.
ADD the lime juice and blend again.
TOSS the hot cooked pasta with the sauce and a bit of cooking water.
SERVE immediately, topped with Parmesan curls if desired.
If using as a dip or dressing, sauce can be held at room temperature for up to an hour or refrigerated in a covered container for one day. Whisk it back together if it separates.

Yield: 6 servings

Fajita Fiesta

Fiesta night is our favorite! When the fajita craving strikes and firing up the grill just isn't an option, fire up the iron skillet and stir fry a sizzling blend of tender chicken and colorful vegetables. This quick and easy taste of the Southwest only looks difficult to make. Spicing the dish with pure ancho chile powder is key and if you're looking for a smoky spice, you can also add a dash of chipotle powder. Just before you carry your skillet to the trivet on the table, squeeze on the lime. Your kitchen will instantly transform into a cantina! Dress your fajitas up the way you like, and be sure to recruit many hands to assemble the festive buffet.

- 1 tablespoon olive oil
- ½ red bell pepper, sliced into thin strips
- ½ green bell pepper, sliced into thin strips
- 1 medium onion, thinly sliced
- 1 pound boneless chicken breast, thinly sliced crosswise
- 2 cloves garlic, crushed or minced
- 1 tablespoon ancho chile powder
- ¼ teaspoon chipotle chile powder (optional)
- ½ teaspoon ground cumin
- 1 teaspoon salt
- Ground pepper
- Juice of 1 lime

For serving:
- Warm flour tortillas
- Shredded cheese
- Jalapeño slices
- Lime wedges
- Sour cream
- Guacamole
- Rainbow Coleslaw is a great topping (see the 'Great Salads' chapter)

HEAT oil in large skillet over medium heat.
ADD red and green bell peppers and onion and stir fry until beginning to soften, about 5 minutes.
TRANSFER to a large bowl using tongs and return skillet to heat.
ADD chicken, garlic, ancho chile and optional chipotle powder, ground cumin and salt and pepper and stir-fry a few minutes until chicken is opaque.
ADD the onion-pepper mixture to the chicken and continue cooking until chicken is done, and peppers are heated through.
SQUEEZE in the juice of 1 lime and toss to combine.
SERVE, buffet style, spooning chicken and peppers into tortillas, and topping as desired.

Ground Beef 'Starter' and 'Taco Meat'

You get three crowd-pleasing meals in one with this versatile 'starter'. Cook once, and with a few embellishments this lightly seasoned ground beef mixture is ready to tweak: Add Asian flavors to one-third of the 'starter' to make Asian Noodle Bowl. The remaining two-thirds gets a Southwestern accent for Inside Out Tacos, and Sloppy Taco Dogs. Recipes follow.

'STARTER' INGREDIENTS
- 1 tablespoon olive oil
- 2 onions, chopped
- 2 cloves garlic, minced
- 2 pounds lean ground beef
- 1 teaspoon salt
- $\frac{1}{4}$ teaspoon pepper

TACO MEAT INGREDIENTS
- 1 tablespoon ancho chili powder
- 1 teaspoon ground cumin
- 1 (14-ounce) can diced tomatoes, preferably 'fire roasted', with juice
- 1 (14-ounce) can black beans, drained and rinsed

HEAT olive oil in a large, deep skillet or Dutch Oven over medium heat.
ADD the onion and sauté until it softens, about 5 minutes.
ADD the garlic and stir 1 minute.
CRUMBLE in the raw beef and break up with a large spoon. ADD the salt and pepper.
STIR occasionally until the meat is no longer pink.
REMOVE one-third of the meat to make 'Asian Noodle Bowl' (see recipe).
MAKE taco meat to create 'Sloppy Taco Dogs' and 'Inside Out Tacos' (see recipes):
ADD chili powder, cumin, and tomatoes to the remaining two-thirds of the meat and stir over medium heat until it just begins to bubble. Reduce heat and simmer until juices are thick.
DIVIDE in half.
ADD prepared beans to half of the taco meat for use in 'Inside-Out Tacos'.

~~~~~~
~~~~~~

A Tip from Aimee – Lean ground beef may cost slightly more per pound, but you have far less loss in the form of liquid fat left in the pan after cooking. It's also better for your heart and waistline. Choose lean!

Ground Beef 'Starter' Recipe #1 - Asian Noodle Bowl

- 12 ounces whole wheat pasta such as Angel Hair or Rotini
- ⅓ of prepared Ground Beef 'Starter' (see recipe)
- 1 tablespoon fresh ginger (peeled, minced)
- 2 tablespoons soy sauce
- Pinch crushed red pepper flakes
- 1 large carrot, peeled and grated
- 3 green onions, thinly sliced
- 1 cup frozen edamame (out of shell)
- 3 tablespoons chopped fresh cilantro
- ¼ cup reserved (hot) pasta cooking water
- Lime wedges

COOK pasta according to package directions, drain and reserve ¼ cup pasta cooking water

HEAT ⅓ reserved ground beef starter in a large skillet over medium-high heat while pasta cooks.

ADD ginger, soy sauce crushed red pepper, carrot, green onions, edamame, and cilantro to pan and stir together to heat through, about 5 minutes.

TOSS with pasta, adding the 1/4 cup reserved cooking water to thin the sauce.

SERVE with lime wedges, if desired.

~~~~~~
~~~~~~

A Tip from Aimee – Mushy noodles no more... Cook pasta al dente (firm and toothsome) and this is better for your health. When noodles are overcooked, the starches (carbohydrates) break down faster during digestion causing spikes in blood sugar levels. Al dente pasta will fuel you longer.

Ground Beef 'Starter' Recipe #2 - Inside Out Tacos

These can be as simple or as elaborate as you like. The concept is to skip the traditional taco shell, using a lettuce leaf in its place. Top your tacos to your liking, and finish them with a sprinkle of crushed tortilla chips on top.

½ recipe of taco meat, with the beans
1 head romaine lettuce, leaves separated, rinsed and dried
Salsa
Guacamole
Reduced fat sour cream
Grated cheddar cheese
Jalapeño pepper slices
A few crushed tortilla chips (or use the end of your tortilla chip bag)

PLACE 3 romaine leaves on each of 4 dinner plates.
DIVIDE the taco meat evenly among the lettuce 'shells'
TOP each with a small spoonful of salsa and guacamole, a little dollop of sour cream, a few shreds of cheddar and a jalapeño slice.
SHOWER each plate with a confetti of crushed tortilla chips.
SERVE.

Yield: 4 servings

Ground Beef 'Starter' Recipe #3 - Sloppy Taco Dogs

There's really nothing to this. Sloppy taco meat in a hot dog bun! Proof of the versatility of the Ground Beef 'Starter'!

- ½ recipe of taco meat (without beans), from Ground Beef 'Starter' recipe
- 4-6 Whole Wheat hot dog buns, heated if desired

SPLIT the buns open without tearing the seam.
SCOOP warmed taco meat into the buns.
SERVE with Rainbow Coleslaw (see recipe in 'Great Salads' chapter).

~~~~~~
~~~~~~

A Tip from Aimee – Check out those buns… Choose whole wheat bread when available and compare the amounts of sodium and sugar…you may be surprised. As a general rule, look for fewer ingredients and those which you can pronounce. Fewer additives in store-bought buns may mean they may become stale sooner so check your expiration or 'packed on' dates to ensure you're getting the freshest product available. Double bag the extra buns and put them in the freezer for next time. Another option? Make bread crumbs (see recipe in the Pantry chapter) or croutons so nothing goes to waste.

Quinoa Pizza

Quinoa is an 'ancient' South American grain that has become wildly popular in the U.S. It is a high-quality protein source that is gluten-free, quick and easy to prepare, and so delicious and versatile! It comes in white, red, and black varieties, each with a different heartiness. It's great as a side dish or a salad, or you can take it way outside the box: Leftover prepared quinoa can be transformed into a pizza crust — more like a pizza casserole, not actually slices you can pick up. Top with sauce, cheese and your favorite pizza toppings — pop it in the oven and serve.

QUINOA WITH SPINACH
- 2 cups water
- ½ teaspoon salt
- 1 cup quinoa, rinsed
- 3 cups fresh spinach leaves, coarsely chopped

QUINOA PIZZA
- Olive oil
- 2 cups prepared quinoa
- 1 cup 'Marinara In Minutes' (see recipe in Pantry chapter)
- 1 cup shredded mozzarella cheese
- Pizza toppings, as desired: Thinly sliced mushrooms • Fresh spinach leaves•Pepperoni slices

QUINOA PREPARATION
BRING water and salt to boil in a medium saucepan.
STIR in quinoa, reduce heat to simmer and cover.
COOK until most of liquid is absorbed and the grains appear to have 'popped' open, about 15 -20 minutes.
REMOVE from heat and gently stir in spinach
COVER for a few minutes to wilt spinach.
SERVE, or use to make Quinoa Pizza.

QUINOA PIZZA PREPARATION
PREHEAT oven to 375 degrees.
BRUSH a 9-inch glass pie dish lightly with olive oil.
SPREAD prepared quinoa evenly in dish to form a 'crust'.
TOP with sauce, spreading to the edge.
SPRINKLE with cheese and add toppings, as desired.
BAKE until cheese is melted and a little golden on top, about 20-25 minutes,
COOL slightly, then cut into wedges and serve.

Yield: 6-8 servings

Roast Chicken

Popping a whole chicken into your oven for an hour or so to roast perfumes your whole house with the fragrance of home cooking. It's a call to the table setters to come to the kitchen and break bread. I love to roast a chicken on Sundays and create encore dishes with the leftovers during the week. Few things are as easy or as satisfying.

- 1 whole chicken, 4 to 5 pounds
- 2 teaspoons coarse salt
- $\frac{1}{2}$ teaspoon ground pepper

Optional:
- Olive oil for brushing
- Lemon wedges

HEAT the oven to 425 degrees.
REMOVE the chicken from its packaging, and remove and reserve the packet of giblets inside the chicken cavity (if there is one).
RINSE the chicken inside and out and pat dry with paper towels.
PLACE the chicken, breast side up, in a large oven-proof skillet, small roasting pan, or Pyrex baking dish.
BRUSH with olive oil, if desired, and season the chicken inside and out with salt and pepper.
SQUEEZE the lemon wedges (2 or 3) inside the cavity and toss the rinds inside as well.
ROAST for 15 minutes.
REDUCE the oven heat to 375 degrees and continue roasting an additional 50 minutes to one hour, until chicken is golden and when slightly tilted, the cavity juices run out clear.
REMOVE from the oven, then let rest about 5 minutes.
TRANSFER to a serving platter. Carve and serve.*

*When carving a whole chicken, reserve the bones and set aside along with the neck from the cavity packet to make stock for soup (see stock recipe in the 'Pantry' chapter). Wrap and refrigerate for up to 3 days or freeze for 3 months.

Yield: 4 servings + leftovers

Roast Chicken Lettuce Wraps

I'm not sure what's better – Roast Chicken Night or all the encore opportunities that follow! When leftover roasted chicken is at the ready, you can assemble these delicious 'wraps' in a hurry! The key is pulling the remaining chicken from the bones immediately after dinner. Stash it in the fridge and then you have lovely bits of tender chicken ready to go for tomorrow. And while you sleep, you can make a luscious pot of stock. See the 'Pantry' chapter for stock success.

- 2 teaspoons canola oil
- $1/2$ yellow onion, vertically sliced
- 1 large clove garlic, crushed
- 1-inch piece fresh ginger, peeled and finely chopped
- $1\,1/2$ cups diced cooked chicken
- 2 tablespoons soy sauce
- 2 tablespoons rice wine vinegar
- Pinch of red pepper flakes
- 1 large carrot, shredded
- 2 cups cooked brown rice
- 2 green onions, thinly sliced
- 4 Bibb/Boston lettuce leaves, rinsed and dried

Optional protein stretchers:
- Frozen edamame (out of shell)
- Sesame seeds

HEAT the oil in a large skillet over medium heat.
ADD the onion and sauté for 5 minutes. Reduce heat to low and add the garlic and ginger and sauté for 1 minute.
ADD chicken, soy sauce, vinegar, pepper flakes, carrot and rice (add edamame, if using) and cook a few minutes to heat through.
STIR in the green onions.
DIVIDE mixture equally among lettuce leaves and sprinkle with sesame seeds, if desired.

Alternative serving suggestions:
Chicken mixture can be served over a bed of salad greens.
Mu-shu chicken? Roll the chicken mixture into small flour tortillas for a dinner on the run.

Yield: 4 servings

Skillet Lasagna

Take a stroll to the 'Pantry' chapter and make some fresh ricotta and marinara (in minutes!). Then you can effortlessly assemble an easy and unforgettable lasagna. Growing up, lasagna was a big deal and seemed to take all afternoon to put it together. Waiting for it to finally emerge from the oven was an event: bubbling sauce meets gooey cheese and tender pasta. With just a few minutes at the stove you can enjoy this same theatre with a lot less fuss. This recipe is your canvas to add your signature: colorful vegetables, fresh herbs, spicy sausage. Very tweakable and certainly a dish you'll perform again and again.

- 3 cups Marinara in Minutes (see the 'Pantry' chapter)
- 12 ounces fettuccini, cooked al dente
- 1 cup ricotta cheese (see recipe in 'Pantry' chapter)

Optional Additions:
- Minced fresh parsley or basil
- Handful of fresh spinach leaves
- 6 ounces cooked Italian sausage
- Parmesan cheese

HEAT the marinara in a large skillet over medium heat until it bubbles and is heated through.

ADD the cooked fettuccini to the sauce in the skillet, using tongs to coat the pasta with the sauce.

ADD desired additions.

SPOON the ricotta over the pasta, dropping it here and there, stirring gently to partially incorporate.

REMOVE from the heat and cover the skillet to melt the cheese for a minute or two.

TOSS a salad and dinner is ready!

Yield: 4-6 servings

Veggie Burgers

A few minutes of prep leads to crazy-good burgers that are packed with
veggie goodness. Serve them on a bun with your choice of toppings, or knife-
and-fork style atop a bed of salad greens.

- 6 ounces fresh mushrooms, sliced 1/4-inch thick
- 1/2 cup fresh breadcrumbs, preferably whole wheat
- 2 green onions, coarsely chopped
- 1 clove garlic
- 1 (15-ounce) can black beans, drained and rinsed
- 1/2 teaspoon ancho chili powder
- 1/2 teaspoon salt
- 1/4 teaspoon pepper
- 1 egg, beaten
- 1 tablespoon oil or bacon grease for the skillet

Optional serving/topping ingredients:
- 6 buns, split and toasted
- Sliced avocado
- Thinly sliced red onion
- Mayonnaise

HEAT the oven to 400 degrees.

ROAST the sliced mushrooms on a parchment-lined rimmed baking sheet
for 10 minutes.

PLACE the breadcrumbs, green onions and garlic in the container of a food
processor and pulse to chop garlic.

ADD the roasted mushrooms, black beans, ancho chili powder, salt, and
pepper and pulse 3 or 4 times until mixture is blended but not pureed. If
large pieces remain, scrape down the side of the processor and pulse one
more time.

TRANSFER the mixture to a bowl and stir in the beaten egg.

FORM the mixture by heaping 1/3 cupfuls into 6 patties, about 3/4-inch thick.
Place them on waxed paper until all are formed. (Can be made 1 day ahead.
Cover and chill until ready to cook).

HEAT the oil in a 10-12-inch skillet (preferably cast iron) over medium heat.

COOK the patties for 3 to 4 minutes per side, until outsides are lightly
crisped and they are cooked through. (Will take a few minutes longer if
patties were chilled).

SERVE and top as desired.

Yield: 6 servings

6

PANTRY

BREADCRUMBS

CHICKEN STOCK

CROSTINI

MARINARA IN MINUTES

RICOTTA

SLOW COOKER BEANS

WHIPPED CREAM

VEGETABLE STOCK

Basics for the Pantry...

These kitchen essentials are the building blocks of easy weeknight meals. With a little advance planning you can stock your freezer and fridge and be on your way to cooking success.

Pull some stock from the freezer and you are moments away from comforting soups from scratch.

A day-old baguette can be thinly sliced then frozen. Pop the slices in the oven for quick crostini. Make homemade breadcrumbs to get the most out of your loaf of good bread.

If you've never made fresh ricotta, try it and you will be converted! Keep some on hand to pair with marinara from the freezer and you can quickly assemble a delicious skillet lasagna. Or spread on crostini, drizzle with honey, and sprinkle with chopped almonds for a satisfying snack.

Create your own family favorites using these basics and you're on your way to cooking success.

Breadcrumbs

A kitchen essential. You can use for meatballs, hand-breaded fish fillets and pork cutlets, chicken and eggplant parmesan, and so many recipes.

Breadcrumbs are a cinch to make using the tail end of your good loaves of bread. I tend to stick with classic homestyle wheat or country white so the crumbs are unflavored from the start. I add the seasonings to harmonize with the recipe. Garlic, herbs, lemon zest and parmesan cheese are my go-tos, but sometimes you simply need 'plain breadcrumbs.' You just 'puree' fresh bread for soft crumbs, the perfect addition to give moisture to your meatballs.

For dry bread crumbs, toast some 'day old' bread and let it get very dry (you can put the bread on a cookie sheet in a hot oven that has been turned off...just don't forget it's in there. When the bread is very dry and crisp-it will 'snap' when you break it in half it is ready to be made into crumbs. You can put a few broken slices into the food processor and let the machine puree it into fine crumbs. OR you can use the fine holes of a grater to scrape it into crumbs. Work on a large cutting mat so the crumbs don't go all over the kitchen! Now that you have these wonderful crumbs, you can keep them in the freezer so you will have lots of delicious breadcrumbs for future recipes. And you'll be able to savor literally every last crumb of your good loaf of bread.

- Bread - as described above

For seasoned bread crumbs, use any of the following according to your taste and to harmonize with the recipe you are using:
- Garlic
- Herbs
- Lemon zest
- Parmesan cheese

TEAR the bread into a few pieces and place in a food processor.
BLEND until crumbly with no large pieces remaining.
STORE in the freezer.

Crostini

What's better than ripping a fresh baguette apart and enjoying it caveman style? Crostini. Essentially crunchy homemade crackers that you can easily bake if you have any baguette remaining the day after it was baked.

I call it bread management – farmers have harvested, bakers have toiled, and you have spent your hard-earned cash for good bread. Grab your bread knife (an absolute kitchen essential!), slice, brush with olive oil, and bake. Enjoy with your favorite spreads!

• Baguette
• Olive oil

HEAT oven to 375 degrees.
SLICE your baguette into ⅓-inch slices – slice them straight across for small crostini, or at long angles for longer slices.
PLACE on a parchment-lined baking sheet.
BRUSH with a little bit of olive oil on the top side.
BAKE for 15-20 minutes, turning over after 10 minutes. Timing will depend on how thin and how crunchy you like your crostini.

Marinara in Minutes

Sure, you can buy any number of jarred 'spaghetti sauces' but try this recipe and you'll be converted to homemade in an instant. Step up to the stove and master a quick marinara. Canned, crushed tomatoes are the secret to marinara magic and I always keep a supply of my favorite brand on hand. I like to make it in big batches and keep the extra in the freezer (straight-sided mason jars are the ticket here). Once the onion hits the hot oil in your pot, the fragrance will wander, beckoning the helpers to the kitchen. Adding a little grated carrot brings sweet harmony to the sauce and a short simmer is all it needs.

You have sauce for meatballs, spaghetti night, your special eggplant parmesan and of course a tempting skillet lasagna.

- 1 tablespoon olive oil
- 1 onion, finely chopped
- 4 cloves garlic, crushed or minced
- 1 carrot, peeled and finely grated
- 2 cans (28-ounce each) crushed tomatoes
- $\frac{1}{2}$ teaspoon dried oregano
- $\frac{1}{2}$ teaspoon salt, or to taste
- $\frac{1}{4}$ teaspoon ground pepper

HEAT the olive oil in a large saucepan over medium heat.
ADD the onion and cook for 7-10 minutes until almost soft, stirring occasionally.
ADD the garlic and carrot and stir 1 minute.
STIR in the tomatoes and oregano and bring to a boil over medium high heat.
REDUCE heat to low and simmer for 15 minutes, stirring occasionally.
SEASON with salt and pepper and let cool before transferring to jars.
MAKES about $6\frac{1}{2}$ cups.

~~~~~~
~~~~~~

A Tip from Aimee – Shop smart. Find healthy brands you like and stick with them. Just make sure to revisit your faves every few months and compare them to similar products at the store. There is always something new and different on grocery shelves. Manufacturers also change their recipes or discontinue products from time to time. Stay flexible and stay informed.

Ricotta

Making your own ricotta is easy and a fascinating project to do with your kids. My friends at J.Q. Dickinson Salt-Works bottle the liquid that remains once their salt crystals take form. This is called nigari. It's a mineral-rich by-product of the salt-making process and is added to heated milk to make ricotta. Once your ricotta has magically cultured with the nigari, and you quietly drain it to remove the excess liquid, you have something otherworldly at your fingertips. Creamy goodness, rich with calcium, so satisfying smeared on a crostini or tossed with hot pasta ala Skillet Lasagna. Make this and you, too, will be hooked.

- ½ gallon of whole milk (raw, or low-heat pasteurized work best)
- ½ teaspoon coarse salt, plus more to finish
- 1 teaspoon of J.Q. Dickinson Salt-Works nigari, plus more if needed

HEAT milk in a heavy bottomed, straight-sided sauce pan with the salt over medium-high heat. Stir gently to dissolve the salt and cook until it reaches 190 degrees.

REMOVE from the heat.

ADD 1 teaspoon of nigari and stir well with a slotted spoon. Watch closely for the milk to start curdling. If nothing happens after 15 seconds or so, then add an additional ½ teaspoon of nigari and stir well.

ADD additional nigari as needed by the ½ teaspoonful until the milk curdles. The freshness of the milk, pasteurization method and whether or not it is homogenized will all affect the amount of nigari needed.

COVER the pan after it curdles and let it sit for 10 minutes to fully separate curds from the whey*.

LINE a strainer with 3 layers of damp cheesecloth over a large bowl.

MOVE the curds gently into the strainer using a slotted spoon. Pour the whey through the cheesecloth/strainer being careful not to break up the curds. Let the curds drain for 20 minutes.

ENJOY immediately or refrigerate for up to 3 days.

*Save your whey. There are many ways to use it from feeding plants in your garden, adding additional nutrition to your pet's meals, and using it as liquid to cook beans or grits.

Yield: About 1½ cups

Slow Cooker Beans

Of course I keep cans of beans in my pantry as an instant addition to my menus, but it's hard to beat the taste, texture, and value of home-cooked beans. A pound of most types of dried beans cooks up into the equivalent of about four cans of beans, so once you cook them, you can cool them and divide them into containers and freeze them for later.

Each variety has variations in cooking times. Black, Great Northern, and Pinto beans cook into perfect tenderness in about four to five hours in your slow cooker. Firmer chick peas take longer. Make them on a Sunday and you have beans ready for the week ahead, hands-off.

- 1 pound dried beans
- 2 quarts water
- 1 1/2 teaspoons salt

PICK over the dried beans to remove any unwanted debris.
RINSE the beans well in a colander and transfer to the casserole of your slow cooker.
ADD the water and salt and turn the cooker to high.
COOK the beans for 4 hours and check their tenderness. If they are cooked through, they are done. If they are still firm, continue checking at 30 minute intervals until they are tender but not mushy.
SERVE or store in their own liquid, refrigerated for up to 5 days or in the freezer for up to 6 months.

Yield: 12 1/2-cup servings

Stock Options – A Concept

"It's all about the broth," says my husband. When you're making soup or a pan sauce, homemade stock is hard to beat. Stock/Broth, the words are nearly interchangeable. In a restaurant kitchen, maybe the stocks are a bit more concentrated. At home, if I need a true 'stock' I reduce my homemade broth to about half its original volume....but, I rarely do this, as it's just not necessary.

True confessions – I keep 'boxed' broth on hand for emergency use, but it's a far cry from the real thing. Besides, you can make nurturing chicken and vegetable stocks with things that would likely end up in the trash can.

If you have a crockpot, you can make chicken stock while you sleep, or you can make the stock on the stovetop (not recommended for while you sleep!). The following pages show you how.

Once you have your wealth of stock, you are moments from delicious soups from scratch – turn to the 'Soup and Bread' chapter for inspiration.

Stock Options – Chicken Stock While You Sleep

Once you have roasted a chicken and enjoyed the delicious meat, you are on your way to easy stock. Just add a quartered onion, a roughly chopped carrot and stalk of celery and a smashed clove of garlic...

Using a crockpot, it can cook while you sleep. If you don't have a crock pot, you can make the stock on the stovetop.

- Roasted chicken carcass
- 1 medium onion, quartered
- 1 carrot, roughly chopped
- 1 stalk of celery, roughly chopped
- 1 clove garlic, smashed
- 3-4 quarts water

CROCKPOT DIRECTIONS

PLACE the bones from your roasted chicken into your crock pot – often there's a small amount of meat still clinging to the bones and that's great. ADD the vegetables and 3-4 quarts of water (amount of water depends on the size of your chicken; you want the chicken to be covered with water). COVER and set it on low for an overnight simmer and in the morning... STRAIN the stock through a fine strainer into a large heat-proof bowl or pot. COOL, then refrigerate or freeze until needed. For ease of use, freeze stock in pint containers so the entire batch does not have to be thawed out. Straight-sided mason jars are great for this!

WHILE YOU'RE AWAKE DIRECTIONS

PLACE all the ingredients into a large stock pot and bring just to a boil then turn down the heat until it just simmers. SIMMER for 1 to 3 hours, depending on your schedule and the strength of stock you desire. SKIM any foam from the top with a spoon and strain and store as above.

Stock Options – Vegetable Stock

Cooking vegetable trimmings overnight in the crock pot isn't necessary for a full-flavored stock. Whenever I'm prepping celery, peeling carrots, cutting onions, or any other vegetables or herbs (parsley, basil, and cilantro stalks!!), I save the scraps and toss them in a freezer bag. When a one-gallon bag is pretty full of these trimmings, I cook them in a pot of water with any extra things I'd like to add. Strain and you're done. This is a pretty effortless way to make a savory stock and is a great base for vegetarian soups.

- Gallon bag of vegetable trimmings
- A few mushrooms
- Some leek greens
- A clove or two of garlic
- Whole peppercorns
- 1 gallon of water

Optional addition:
- Celery seed

PUT your gallon bag of vegetable trimmings and the rest of the vegetables in a stockpot with 1 gallon of water, plus a few mushrooms, some leek greens, a clove or two of garlic, a sprinkle of peppercorns, and some celery seed if you have it.

BRING to a boil, then reduce heat and simmer one hour.

STRAIN the stock through a fine strainer into a large heat-proof bowl or pot.

COOL, then refrigerate or freeze until needed.

Whipped Cream

A little dollop of freshly whipped cream is an unforgettable accent to your homemade desserts. I vividly remember the first time I whipped a little half-pint carton of cream, watching the twin beaters spin the thick cream from liquid to fluff in magical minutes. Just add air and your cream holds tall peaks. In my youth, I was following a recipe from a magazine which called for 'whipped topping.' My mother refused to buy the frozen tub of topping, citing its ingredients list, none of which was actually cream.

Start with fresh, very cold cream, and be sure to chill your bowl and beaters to get perfectly whipped cream every time. Stop the mixer once you have soft peaks – the cream will whip itself into butter if you beat too long.

Note: You can also whisk cream into beautiful fluff with a whisk, a fun way to discreetly flex your kitchen prowess.

- 1 cup heavy or whipping cream, very cold
- 1 tablespoon granulated sugar
- $\frac{1}{2}$ teaspoon vanilla extract

POUR the cream into a deep narrow bowl, preferably a metal bowl that has been chilled, along with the beaters of a hand-mixer (or a whisk).
BEAT on low speed with the hand mixer (or high speed with your whisk in hand) until beginning to thicken.
BEAT or whisk in the sugar and vanilla until soft peaks form.
SERVE immediately.

Yield: 2 cups

Notes

7

APPLE PIE SUNDAES

BEST. BROWNIES. EVER.

CHOCOLATE GODDESS CUPCAKES

COOKIE CAKE

ESPRESSO BLONDIES

PERSONAL PEACH PIES

SUNSHINE CITRUS PIE

THREE COOKIES IN ONE

A Little Sugar and Spice...

I have tackled my share of 'cake projects' for special celebrations, but these recipes are my favorites. Delicious classics, some with a twist, served in personal portions.

When you want a little something sweet, these treats can be made fuss-free for any occasion.

These are just as easy as reaching for a boxed mix, but you can truly taste the difference. Keep your baking pantry well-stocked and add some seasonal fruit and you'll be effortlessly baking from scratch.

Apple Pie Sundaes

You can enjoy this with a spoon, or casually carve into your ice cream with one of your cinnamon crisps, scooping up a tender spiced apple with each bite. Cinnamon Tortilla Chips + Apple Pie Apples + Ice Cream =YUM! In our town we have a favorite scoop shop, Ellen's Homemade. Her ice cream takes these sundaes to the next level.

- 1 tablespoon granulated sugar
- $\frac{1}{2}$ teaspoon ground cinnamon
- 4 8-inch flour tortillas
- 1 tablespoon butter, melted

- 2 medium apples, peeled, cored, and sliced (about $\frac{3}{4}$-inch thick slices)
- $\frac{1}{4}$ cup packed light brown sugar
- $\frac{1}{2}$ teaspoon ground cinnamon
- $\frac{1}{4}$ teaspoon coarse salt
- 1 tablespoon butter
- Vanilla ice cream (good quality - if in Charleston, Ellen's is our go-to!)

FOR CINNAMON TORTILLA CHIPS:
HEAT the oven to 375 degrees.
COMBINE sugar and cinnamon in a small bowl.
BRUSH tortillas with melted butter. Lightly sprinkle with cinnamon mixture.
CUT each into 8 wedges and arrange in single layer on a parchment-lined baking sheet.
BAKE for about 10 minutes or until golden brown and crisp. Let cool on sheet before eating.
STORE extra 'chips' in an airtight container for up to 1 week.

FOR APPLE PIE APPLES:
STIR together the apple slices and brown sugar in a medium skillet over medium-low heat.
COOK for about 10 minutes, stirring occasionally, until apples are tender.
ADD cinnamon, salt, and butter, and stir gently until butter melts. Serve hot or cold.

TO ASSEMBLE SUNDAES:
PLACE one scoop of vanilla ice cream into each of 4 dessert dishes.
SPOON some warm apples onto each, dividing evenly.
TOP with a few crispy tortilla triangles.

Best. Brownies. Ever.

This is a tall claim, but in my vast experience of brownie tasting and testing, these win – especially if you factor in the no-fuss recipe! In our kitchen, there's the baking area that my husband calls 'the chocolate station.' We don't keep much candy around, but the chocolate for baking is usually in good supply. Everyone loves visiting the chocolate station, taking a little discreet nibble of this or that. Sometimes I go there and my supply has vanished! So I keep a bag of chocolate chips hidden away... I love, love, love big crunchy walnuts in each brownie bite. Up to you, nuts or no. Find the easy pan-prep instructions in the 'Smart Kitchen' chapter.

- ⅓ cup butter
- ¾ cup sugar
- 2 tablespoons water
- 2 cups semi-sweet chocolate chips, divided (I prefer the bittersweet)
- 2 eggs
- 1 teaspoon vanilla
- ¾ cup all-purpose flour
- ¼ teaspoon salt
- ¼ teaspoon baking soda
- ½ cup chopped nuts, optional (preferably toasted)

HEAT oven to 325 degrees.
BUTTER and flour a 9" square pan.
MELT butter, sugar, and water together in a large microwavable glass bowl. Microwave on high for about 1 minute, until butter is melted.
WHISK to combine and heat for about 1 minute longer, until bubbling.
WHISK in 1 cup chocolate chips and stir until melted. Let cool slightly (so eggs won't scramble).
ADD eggs and vanilla and whisk until thoroughly combined.
STIR in flour, baking soda, salt, nuts, and remaining 1 cup chocolate chips.
STIR until flour is thoroughly incorporated.
SPREAD batter in prepared pan, and bake until the top is puffed, shiny, and cracked, about 30 minutes.
COOL completely in pan on rack.
CUT into squares and serve.
DID YOU KNOW??
Cutting warm brownies with a plastic knife works like a charm – no sticky crumbs.

Yield: 16 2-inch squares, or 32 triangles

Chocolate Goddess Cupcakes

Extraordinary chocolate cake is so easy there's no need to use a boxed cake mix. Melt some butter, add brown sugar, whisk in an egg, some flour and cocoa. The magical transformation occurs with the addition of a secret ingredient: Coffee. Coffee enhances the subtle richness of the cocoa and makes the cake incredibly moist.

Scoop the batter into muffin pans lined with your choice of fancy cupcake papers, pop them in the oven and you're on your way to baking goddess.

- 1 cup unbleached flour
- ⅓ cup unsweetened cocoa powder
- ½ teaspoon baking soda
- ½ teaspoon baking powder
- ½ teaspoon coarse salt
- ½ cup butter (1 stick)
- 1 cup packed brown sugar
- ¼ cup milk
- 1 egg
- 1 teaspoon vanilla extract
- ½ cup hot coffee

HEAT the oven to 350 degrees.

LINE a regular-sized muffin pan with 12 cupcake liners.

WHISK the flour, cocoa powder, baking soda, baking powder, and salt together in a bowl.

MELT the butter in a medium saucepan over low heat. Stir in the brown sugar.

WHISK the milk, egg, and vanilla extract together in a small bowl and add to the butter and sugar, stirring to combine.

ADD the flour mixture and whisk just to combine (mixture will be thick).

STIR in the hot coffee and mix into a nearly-smooth batter.

SCOOP the batter (about ¼-cupfuls) into the prepared muffin pan, dividing evenly.

BAKE for 18-20 minutes until tops are slightly puffed and feel just firm when carefully poked with your fingertip.

REMOVE pan from oven and cool in the pan on a rack for 5 minutes. Carefully turn the cupcakes out and let them continue to cool, right side up, for about 10 minutes.

FILL AND FROST using the instructions that follow.

Yield: 12 cupcakes

Chocolate Goddess Cupcakes - Filling and Frosting

While your cupcakes are baking, you have 20 leisurely minutes to hull some strawberries and whip up some fluffy chocolate cream for the impressive finish.

This is not difficult. On the contrary, it's so simple, it's a go-to for last minute parties, bake sales, or even after-dinner cravings. That's right! This super easy, ultra-delicious recipe will keep you happily occupied at the oven for all upcoming occasions. Get ready for the requests.

Keep some basic baking staples on hand and you're moments from chocolate luxury. Don't just take my word for it, dust off those muffin pans and brace yourself for the onslaught of cupcake praise.

- 12 small strawberries, rinsed, dried, and hulled, plus additional for top garnish (raspberries also work well)
- ¼ cup powdered sugar
- 3 tablespoons cocoa powder
- 1 cup whipping cream
- ½ teaspoon vanilla extract

COMBINE sugar and cocoa in a mixing bowl and whisk to combine.
WHISK in cream gradually.
CHILL mixture for 15 minutes.
ADD vanilla extract to cream mixture.
WHIP using an electric mixer or hand beater, until stiff peaks form. (Super goddess trick: whisk by hand!)
SCOOP a melon-ball size of cupcake out of the center of each cooled cupcake (see previous recipe) and push a small hulled berry inside (raspberries also work well).
PIPE the chocolate cream onto each cupcake and garnish with a whole small berry if desired.
SERVE immediately.

~~~~~~
~~~~~~

A Tip from Aimee – Homemade cupcakes are fun to make, crowd pleasers, and the perfect-size bit of indulgence. These self-contained treats are portion control at its finest. Remember, homemade versions are almost always healthier than store bought varieties. Bake on.

Cookie Cake

This is really not a cake, but the best chocolate chip cookie dough, baked in a large round and simply finished with the message of your choice. "I Love You," "Congratulations" and of course "Happy Birthday". It works for all occasions! We serve this at the finale of summer cooking camp. You don't have to commit to baking it as a giant cookie – the dough is perfect for individual cookies, too.

COOKIE:
- ¾ cup butter, softened
- ½ cup sugar
- ½ cup brown sugar
- 1 egg
- 1 ½ teaspoons vanilla extract
- 1 ¾ cups unbleached flour
- 1 teaspoon baking soda
- ½ teaspoon coarse salt
- ¾ cup quick cooking oats
- 1 ½ cups chocolate chips (reserve some for garnish, if desired)

FROSTING:
- ¼ cup butter, softened
- 1 ⅓ cups powdered sugar
- Pinch of salt
- 2 tablespoons cream
- 1 teaspoon vanilla extract

COOKIE:
HEAT oven to 350 degrees.
BUTTER a 12-inch cake pan or line a rimmed baking sheet with parchment.
CREAM the butter until smooth and mix in the sugars.
BEAT until fluffy and add the egg and vanilla extract, mixing to incorporate egg.
COMBINE the flour, baking soda, salt, and oats in a medium bowl.
ADD the flour mixture gradually to the egg and sugars, mixing to combine.
STIR in the chocolate chips.
PAT the dough into the prepared pan.
BAKE for 15-20 minutes until golden and set in the center.
COOL in pan on a rack before frosting.

FROSTING:
CREAM the butter until smooth and gradually add the powdered sugar and a pinch of salt, scraping the bowl as needed.
MIX in the cream and vanilla extract and beat until fluffy.
TRANSFER the frosting to a piping bag and decorate your cookie creation as desired.

Espresso Blondies

When life got busy when my kids were tiny, I was not sure how I would have time for my cooking habit. Enter the fabulous book, "Bake and Freeze Desserts" by Elinor Klivans, which gives great advice for cooking ahead. This is my version of the original recipe from this fun book. Indeed, the brownies freeze well. I individually wrap them and stash them in the freezer for unexpected dessert emergencies.

- 1 1/2 cups unbleached flour
- 1 teaspoon baking powder
- 3/4 teaspoon salt
- 3/4 cup (1 1/2 sticks) unsalted butter, softened
- 1/2 cup sugar
- 1 cup light brown sugar
- 2 eggs
- 2 tablespoons instant coffee powder dissolved in 2 teaspoons hot water
- 1 teaspoon vanilla extract
- 1 cup chocolate chips

PREHEAT oven to 325 degrees.
BUTTER a 13x9x2-inch baking pan (I line it with foil, helpful but not necessary – see the 'Smart Kitchen'chapter for instructions).
WHISK the flour, baking powder, and salt in a bowl to combine.
CREAM butter on medium speed in the large bowl of an electric mixer.
ADD the sugar and brown sugar and beat until the butter and sugars are fluffy, about 1 minute.
TURN the mixer to low and mix in the eggs, dissolved espresso, and vanilla, just until the eggs are incorporated. The mixture will be lumpy and look curdled (this is ok –overmixing the eggs will make the brownies cake-like instead of chewy).
STOP the mixer and carefully scrape the sides of the bowl once during this mixing.
ADD flour mixture and mix just until the flour is incorporated and the mixture is smooth. Mix in the chocolate chips.
SPREAD the batter evenly in the prepared pan.
BAKE until the edges look slightly firm and the center is still slightly soft, about 28-35 minutes.
LET cool completely, then cut into 12 squares (I cut each square into triangles).

Yield: 12 squares or 24 triangles

Personal Peach Pies

Individual pies highlight the best of summer fruit and a perfect opportunity to visit an orchard near you!

- 1 recipe personal pie crostata dough (see recipe), divided for 12 tiny tarts
- ¼ cup unbleached flour, for rolling the dough
- 3 tablespoons plus 2 teaspoons sugar
- 6 fresh peaches (or plums or nectarines), sliced off the pit into eighths
- 1 tablespoon milk

SPRINKLE a clean work surface with flour, and gently pat each dough disk into the flour to lightly coat.

ROLL out half of the dough disks into 5 to 6-inch circles and transfer each to a parchment-lined baking sheet.

SPRINKLE each circle of dough with ½ teaspoon sugar.

REPEAT with remaining dough onto another lined baking sheet.

KEEP one sheet chilled while you work with the first.

DIVIDE fruit into 12 equal portions.

LAY one portion of peach slices in the center of each dough circle, leaving a 1-inch border, mounding any extra fruit just slightly in center.

FOLD plain edge of crust up to partially enclose peaches, leaving fruit exposed in center. Gently fold and pinch dough edge to seal any cracks. Dough will drape gently over fruit, with creases or folds every few inches enclosing the fruit around the edges.

REPEAT until all tarts are formed. Tarts can be chilled for several hours before baking.

PREHEAT oven to 425 degrees.

BRUSH crust with milk and sprinkle top of fruit and dough with remaining sugar.

BAKE pies until crust is golden brown and fruit is bubbling, 20-25 minutes.

REMOVE from oven.

COOL on baking sheet 10 minutes.

CAN BE MADE 4 hours ahead. Let stand on sheet at room temperature. Rewarm in 425-degree oven 5 minutes before serving.

Note: Recipe can easily be halved. Freeze remaining wrapped dough disks in a freezer zip-top bag.

Yield: 12 personal pies

Personal Pie Crostata Dough

A food processor makes light work of this pastry. If you don't have a food processor, the dough can be mixed by hand.

- 1 cup (2 sticks) cold unsalted butter
- 2 cups unbleached flour
- 3 tablespoons granulated sugar
- $\frac{1}{2}$ teaspoon kosher salt
- $\frac{1}{4}$ cup ice cold water

CUT the butter into $\frac{1}{2}$ inch cubes and keep cold.

PLACE flour, sugar, and salt in the bowl of a food processor fitted with the steel blade. Pulse a few times to combine.

ADD the cold butter cubes to the processor, carefully tossing with a spatula to coat each butter cube with flour (this prevents the butter cubes from sticking together and helps them combine more evenly with the flour)

PULSE 15 times, or until the butter particles are the size of small peas.

ADD the ice water all at once through the feed tube while the motor is running.

PROCESS for about 10 seconds, stopping the machine before the dough becomes a solid mass.

ADD a few sprinkles of cold water and pulse again, If the dough seems dry and crumbly.

TURN the contents of the bowl onto a sheet of parchment paper, pressing any loose particles into the mass of dough. DIVIDE into 12 equal pieces for individual tarts. Roughly form each piece of dough into a disk and wrap in parchment or plastic wrap.

CHILL for at least one hour. The dough may be refrigerated for up to 2 days or frozen for up to 2 weeks.

Yield: Enough dough for 12 individual pies

Sunshine Citrus Pie

Key Lime Pie with a kick! Lime zest in the crust adds a nice twist, and the addition of lemon and orange juices elevates the citrus flavor.

CRUST INGREDIENTS
- 10 full sheets of graham crackers, crushed into crumbs
- 1 tablespoon sugar
- Zest of 1 lime
- ¼ cup butter, melted

OPTIONAL GARNISH FOR FINISHED PIE
- Freshly whipped cream
- Thin slices of citrus

FILLING INGREDIENTS
- 4 egg yolks
- 1 (14-ounce) can sweetened condensed milk
- ⅓ cup fresh squeezed lime juice (from about 2 limes)
- 2 tablespoons fresh squeezed lemon juice
- 2 tablespoons fresh squeezed orange juice

CRUST PREPARATION
HEAT the oven to 350 degrees.
TOSS the graham cracker crumbs in a medium bowl with the sugar and lime zest and stir to combine.
ADD the melted butter and mix until crumbs are evenly moist.
PRESS mixture evenly into a 9-inch pie dish.
BAKE for 8 minutes, or just until fragrant and light golden.
COOL on a rack while you make the filling.
REDUCE oven temperature to 325 degrees.

FILLING PREPARATION
WHISK egg yolks until slightly thick and a shade lighter.
ADD the sweetened condensed milk and stir well.
ADD the lime juice, lemon juice, and orange juice and stir to combine
POUR mixture into cooled crust.
BAKE for 15 minutes.
COOL on a rack
REFRIGERATE until ready to serve
GARNISH with dollops of whipped cream, and citrus slices.
CUT into thin slices and serve.

Yield: 12 delicate slices

Three Cookies in One

For my wedding long ago, my aunt gave us an unforgettable gift – a collection of seasonings from Penzeys Spices. I'd never heard of Penzeys but I quickly got acquainted and remain a devoted customer. When I travel, I check for a Penzeys store and reload my spice supplies. I also order through their catalog which is filled with stories and recipes from cooks across the country. This cookie recipe was inspired by one in their catalog. I made a few changes and named it Three Cookies in One, because it's just that – a satisfying combination of my three favorite cookies: Chocolate Chip, Peanut Butter, and Oatmeal.

- ½ cup butter (1 stick), softened
- 1 cup peanut butter
- ½ cup sugar
- ½ cup brown sugar, packed
- ¾ teaspoon coarse salt
- 2 eggs
- 1 teaspoon vanilla extract
- ¼ cup PB2 powder*
- 1 teaspoon cinnamon
- 1 teaspoon baking soda

- 3 cups rolled oats
- 1 cup dark chocolate chips
- ½ cup raisins or dried cherries
- ½ cup chopped walnuts

HEAT the oven to 350 degrees.
CREAM the butter and peanut butter together and mix in the sugars and salt.
MIX well and add the eggs, vanilla, PB2 powder, cinnamon and baking soda, mixing to incorporate.
ADD the oats, chocolate chips, raisins, and walnuts and stir to blend.
DROP teaspoonfuls of the dough onto parchment-lined baking sheets about 2 inches apart.
BAKE for 10 minutes until golden (for a chewier cookie) or 12 minutes for crunchy cookies.
COOL on the sheets.

*PB2 is powdered peanut butter, found in the natural foods aisle of most grocery stores. You can omit this but it boosts the peanut flavor and adds a bit of protein.

Yield: About 4 dozen

8

SMART
KITCHEN

CARROT CUTS

ESTIMATING INGREDIENTS

GARLIC MASTER

GRATE SOME CHEESE

NO-MESS BACON

ONIONS WITHOUT TEARS

SMART COFFEE

ROAST YOUR VEGGIES

April's Kitchen Intelligence

I've been playing in the kitchen my whole life, learning new things every time I cook. Any time I have an idle moment, I delve into a cookbook or food magazine to explore new skills and techniques. I love every minute of it!

Cooking becomes second nature and a happy habit when you master a few basics. Here I share some of the most frequently asked questions from my readers and cooking students, and things I've learned along the way.

From measuring to storing to slicing and dicing, the answers are here. Grab your apron, cue up a great playlist, and embrace your kitchen!

FAQs for the Smart Kitchen

Q: What's the best way to use fresh CITRUS in my recipes?
A: Citrus fruits such as lemons, limes, and oranges add bright flavor and a burst of vitamin C to your dishes. The fruits' colorful outer rind contains the flavorful oils. First rinse the fruit before zesting with a microplane or other fine grater. Swipe the fruit just once, then turn it and swipe again as you roll it across the zesting tool. You just want the very top layer before getting any of the bitter white layer beneath. Any unused zest can be wrapped and frozen for up to 6 months. The fruit can then be juiced by hand or with a small press.

Q: My family loves SALADS. Do you recommend packaged salad blends?
A: Prepping your own salad takes just a few minutes of your time and saves money. Also, some of the packaged blends may contain preservatives so it's best to DIY. (Or, if you do buy the packages, be sure to buy whole-leaf varieties and not the pre-chopped salad mixes.) A salad spinner is a kitchen hero! Rinse and spin your sturdier salad greens such as romaine or red/green leaf lettuce, then store them in storage bags in your produce bin. More delicate salad greens should be rinsed and spun shortly before serving.

Q: I love to keep fresh CARROTS on hand since they keep well in my produce drawer. What's the best way to incorporate them into salads and recipes?
A: First rinse or scrub the carrots to clean them, then use a vegetable peeler to remove the top layer of peel. The peels can be kept in a freezer bag for making vegetable stock (see the Vegetable Stock option in the 'Pantry' chapter). Whole carrots can be grated on the large holes of a cheese grater and tossed into salads, or the shredded bits can be used as a salad on their own. Dress to suit your menu. (See the 'Great Salads' chapter.) Carrots can also be cut into long, slender strands with a julienne peeler or into wide ribbons with a regular vegetable peeler. Finely grated carrot melts away into soups and sauces, adding a hint of sweetness without adding sugar.

Q: AVOCADOS are a new family favorite. How do I store them?
A: Avocados ripen at room temperature. As soon as they are slightly soft near the stem end, they are ready to eat, or to be refrigerated for an extra day or two of storing. You can speed up the ripening process by placing the fruit in a small paper bag along with a ripe banana...check it regularly! Otherwise, just keep them in your fruit basket on your counter along with your apples, bananas, oranges, lemons, and limes.

Q: My kids eat the little GRAPE TOMATOES like candy and we've been growing them in our garden. Is there an easy way to cut them in half for salads?

A: Very young kids can easily 'saw' through them with a serrated plastic picnic knife. They can pinch it between their thumb and forefinger and gently saw back and forth with the knife, cutting them in two. These are great for a quick salsa or to add to salads. Another great way that is super quick is to place the grape tomatoes between two deli lids, tops facing each other, and carefully mash the lids together with one hand (use the heel/palm to press down while arching the fingertips upward), then slice through between the lids, cutting the tomatoes in half.

Q: What's the best alternative to steaming FRESH VEGETABLES?

A: Roasting veggies is the way to go! Simple rule of thumb: if you like it steamed, you'll love it roasted! Roasting enhances the flavor and texture of most vegetables. Best bets: broccoli or cauliflower florets, slender green beans, asparagus spears, chunks of potatoes and sweet potatoes, cubes of squash. Toss the chosen bite-size veggie with a little olive oil and a sprinkle of salt and pepper. Roast in a hot oven – 425 degrees or so, until beginning to brown with a crisp exterior and just fork tender (about 15 minutes for broccoli, cauliflower, green beans, and asparagus, and 30-40 minutes for potatoes and squash).

Q: How do I store and prepare ONIONS?

A: To store onions, put them in a cool, dry place like a basket in the pantry. To prepare onions, shave off the root end of the onion with a sharp knife and discard, then cut off the 'sprout' end. Cut the onion in half from end to end and then remove the skin (rinsed onion skins are a great addition to the freezer stock bag). For chopped onion: slice each half cut-side-down without cutting through the root, then slice crosswise while holding together at the root end. For sliced onion: remove the root end and slice thick or thin, following the natural lines of the onion.

Q: I hear GARLIC has some great health benefits. What's the best way to manage a head of fresh garlic?

A: One head of garlic contains about 10 or 15 cloves and it keeps well on the kitchen counter for up to two weeks. A special garlic keeper is nice but not necessary – a small dish is fine. To separate the cloves, place the whole head of garlic, root-side down, on a cutting board and smash it gently with a heavy object such as a can. The cloves will fall away from the head. To peel a clove, gently smash the clove of garlic with the side of a knife and remove the peel.

The garlic can be crushed with a garlic press or minced – cut the clove lengthwise then crosswise into tiny pieces.

Q: Is it OK to use packaged GRATED CHEESES?
A: Grating cheese yourself is the best option! Blocks of cheese are much more flavorful than the pre-shredded types which also contain preservatives and coatings to keep the shreds from sticking together. Grating your own is also more economical. A tall box-style grater is best for softer cheeses like mozzarella, Monterey Jack, and cheddar. For firm cheeses like Parmesan and asiago, a microplane grater is the best tool to use. Parmesan curls can be made with a vegetable peeler.

Q: What are these lovely spicy CHIPOTLES I hear about?
A: Chipotles in adobo are smoked jalapeños – use more than a teaspoon if you love spicy. Chipotles are available in the ethnic section of most grocery stores. Add them to dishes where you'd like a touch of smoky spice. Transfer any leftover chipotles to a small jar and keep for up to 6 months.

Q: What are the best items to keep stocked in my PANTRY?
A: Canned diced and whole plum tomatoes; dried pasta-angel hair, linguine, penne; rice; quinoa; canned beans; artichoke hearts; extra virgin olive oil; sherry vinegar; cider vinegar; yellow onions; heads of fresh garlic.

Q: I'd like to start BAKING from scratch. What can I keep on hand?
A: A well-stocked baking pantry ideally contains unbleached flour and whole wheat flour, granulated sugar, brown sugar, honey, dark chocolate chips, unsweetened cocoa powder, baking soda, non-aluminum baking powder, pure vanilla extract, oats, your favorite nuts. A couple pounds of butter are also good to keep on hand – I keep a couple pounds in the freezer.

Q: What's the best way to measure and soften BUTTER for baking?
A: Butter typically comes in a one-pound box containing 4 sticks. A single stick of butter is equal to ½ cup. The lines on the butter wrapper make measuring easy! To soften, it's best to measure the amount you need, then cut it into thin slices which will soften quickly. Softened butter can be pressed with your fingertip without being melty-soft.

Q: What do you think about ESTIMATING a measurement?
A: When you are cooking on the stove, you can estimate the tablespoon or two of oil, as you will save on cleanup of the measuring spoons. When you are baking, measurements need to be more accurate as the results are based on the chemical reactions of the ingredients.

Q: What's the best way to store and to measure FLOUR?
A: Flour keeps well in an airtight canister in your baking area. To measure, stir the flour in the canister to loosen it, then spoon it to overflowing in your 'dry' measuring cup, without packing it (very important!). Scrape a straight edge across the top to level it off. Measuring over a sheet of wax paper makes for easy clean-up.

Q: How do I prepare my BAKING PANS for my scratch baking?
A: Turn your baking pan upside down and place a large sheet of foil, shiny side down, on the pan. Fold the foil up on each side to make a perfect mold that's the shape of the pan. Turn the pan right side up and place the foil mold inside, lifting the edges to fit inside the pan. Next rub the pan with a little soft butter. This makes cutting brownies a breeze, just lift the edge of the foil and slide the cooled bar onto a cutting board. Cookie sheets can be lined with a sheet of parchment paper for no-stick cookies and easy clean-up.

Q: Which spices are most commonly used for a SPICE RACK?
A: Essential spices include ancho chile powder, black peppercorns, ground cumin, dried oregano, cinnamon, ground ginger, curry powder, and coarse salt. I prefer to create my own spice blends so I can control the type and amount of salt (many blends on store shelves are loaded with processed salt).

Q: Are there things I can keep IN THE FRIDGE so I'm ready to cook?
A: Keeping these staple items on hand is key! Skim milk, eggs, Dijon mustard, soy sauce, plain yogurt, light sour cream, romaine lettuce, whole carrots, fresh herbs (flat leaf parsley keeps well and is so versatile), unsalted butter, a block of cheddar cheese, and a wedge of Parmesan cheese.

Q: Now that we have cut back on eating frozen meals, our FREEZER is nearly empty! How can I stock it with good things to help with my cooking success?
A: With all that free space you can keep plenty of great things on hand! Frozen fruits and berries are great for making smoothies (visit U-pick orchards in the summer and freeze your harvest!, or buy fruit in bulk during peak season at your farmer's market or produce store, then bag and freeze in usable quantities). Buying meats in bulk from local farms is often economical and great for filling a freezer. Whole chickens for roasting and boneless chicken breasts are also great to keep on hand. Also, don't forget your gallon bag of vegetable trimmings for stock, and freezing your containers of homemade stock and slow cooker beans. (See 'Pantry' chapter for recipes.)

Q: What's the best way to cook BACON? We don't eat it often, but enjoy it occasionally on the weekends.
A: Cooking bacon in the oven is efficient and saves on clean-up. For the quickest cooking, cut the slices crosswise in half and bake at 425 degrees on a parchment-lined rimmed baking sheet for about 20 minutes, turning over halfway through cooking. Drain on paper towels and store any extra slices in the refrigerator.

Q: I often have COFFEE left over in the morning. Is there a way to keep it?
A: A great smart coffee drink is to freeze your leftover coffee in ice cube trays. Pop the frozen cubes into freezer bags and make your own iced coffee drinks. Saves time, money, and calories!

Q: How do I care for my CAST IRON cookware?
A: Gently scrub your pan, once it has cooled, with running water and a soft scrubbing sponge. Dry the pan over a low burner just until water droplets are dry. Set a timer for 5 minutes so you remember. If the pan needs to be re-seasoned, rub the clean, hot pan with a small wad of paper towel and a few drops of cooking oil.

Q: Do I need a large set of fancy KNIVES? Stores usually sell big knife collections for much less than buying them individually.
A: The most often-used knives are a 6 or 8-inch chef's knife, a 3 or 4-inch paring knife, and a serrated bread knife. You can actually save money by buying just the knives you are most likely to use on a regular basis.

Notes

Thank You!

ACKNOWLEDGMENTS

As with any project, many hands make the work light. With the help of so many talented and generous hands, this book has become a reality. I am truly grateful for all the support! I would not have endeavored into writing a book without the encouraging nudge from Sara who urged, "Mom, write a cookbook! I'll help you." Everyone can be grateful to Sara for limiting my exclamation points.

THANK YOU

- Charles for bringing home the bacon and keeping the knives sharp, and for being a great cooking partner
- Our daughters Sara, Reilly, and Emma for being exceptional kitchen helpers
- Mom for always encouraging us in the kitchen and for so many fabulous family dinners
- Dad for always blessing our food and our table
- My whole family and all the extensions for amazing shared meals and kitchen experiences
- Lisa Wallace, editor extraordinaire – this book would still be in its infancy without your partnership and persistence
- Aimee Henry, RDN for a lifetime of kitchen fun and for sharing your nutrition expertise – your words help shape the focus of this book
- Sean Hyde for stepping in and saving the day
- Sally Barton for the beautiful artisan-made props
- John and Cynthia Barrett for sharing your beautiful kitchen
- Vincent Hamilton for being a great sounding board
- The Charleston Gazette for offering a weekly platform for my cooking message
- My Bedford neighborhood for your generous support
- Molly O'Neill for shouting "You can do it!" and helping guide my pen
- My Cook N Scribble tribe for supportive feedback
- MESH Design for the cover design and chapter introduction design
- To the folks at Heritage Cookbook for their great platform
- All the supporters who contributed financially through Indiegogo

All photographs are by April Hamilton except Roast Chicken by Steve Payne and Buckwheat Noodle Salad by Kenny Kemp

Index

APRIL HAMILTON is a cooking instructor and a food writer and photographer. She shares her easy, practical recipes for delicious food through her cooking classes for kids, families, and corporations, and through her weekly column in the Charleston Gazette. Visit her on her blog, www.AprilsKitchenCounter.com. April's husband and three daughters help with testing and tasting in their Charleston, West Virginia kitchen.
This is her first cookbook.

AIMEE HENRY is a Personal Chef and Registered Dietitian Nutritionist – see her nutrition tips throughout the book. She believes food and healthy eating does not have to be complicated. With just a little nutrition information and skill development in the kitchen, healthy and satisfying meals are just a plate away. Aimee is committed to helping people find a wholesome balance of foods to achieve personal health and wellness goals. Aimee lives and works in Denver, Colorado and is a longtime (childhood) foodie friend of April Hamilton.